You're Not Crazy, You're Awakening

Journey To Discovering Your Soul Purpose, Joy And Abundant Life

Rev. Dr. Edwige Bingue

What People are Saying...

"Edwige is a rare combination of collective consciousness and action. She is a natural healing force. In her presence I experienced a lifting up, a joy delivered with such grace and compassion, I didn't realize the full impact until hours later. She is a true Master devoted to serving all."

GREGORY C. JOSEPH, INTERNATIONALLY ACCLAIMED INTUITIVE, HEALER

"Thank you Edwige, for all you've done for me. When I started having ascension symptoms I was afraid. The day my leg 'disappeared' I thought I was having a stroke. Then I found your class, 'You're Not Crazy, You're Awakening.'"

Everything you've shared has taught me so much. The violet flame prayer helped me with more than my fear. I use it daily to transmute everything negative. Transmuting the fear reawakened the God given gifts I had as a child. All my separate selves are coming into alignment. I physically feel my third eye opening. Your guided meditations took me into my heart for the first time. What a joy! My aura photograph showed my aura changed to a bright blue and green, and, all my chakras are open and active.

You also taught me the Merkaba activation meditation. There are times I can actually see the ring of light. I am also manifesting. Amazing! I'm so blessed to have you in my life. In fact, the whole world is blessed to have you with us. Thank you with all my heart. I love you."

SHELLY FAY, LAS VEGAS, NV

"I received coaching from Dr. Edwige Bingue, and, it was amazing how quickly and easily my goals manifested, soared and executed. I learned meditation and how to BREATHE which was KEY for me. My dreams became my reality…I consider her to be one of my "Modern Day Gurus"… The day I met her I felt as if I've known her a lifetime ago…..Forever Grateful.. Angels do walk on this earth…."

RAQUEL STEWART, REIKI MASTER, LAS VEGAS, NV

"I've known Dr. Edwige Bingue since 2009. In 2011 both Edwige and I attended the wedding of a friend. Approaching her, I felt an energy of light, love and a deep commitment to connecting with the each person she encounters. As I walked closer the stronger the energy became. I became focused and present of me, aware of my I AM presence. That perfect power which flows through every being.

The flow of energy brought me to a field of unconscious awareness. as if a veil lifted.. I became present to my breath and an observer of self. Edwige and I greeted each other with hugs. Stepping back from our embrace, I noticed flashing white lights around her head. She had a flashing crown on her head. I was in a trance as though the lights dancing around her head activated something inside. Without prior experience to compare; I chose to become an observer. Edwige noticed I was experiencing something. She lovingly asked, "Are you alright dear? Is there something wrong?"

I replied, "You have lights flashing around your head. Something is happening."
Edwige smiled and said, "Yes I know. Would you like to talk about it?"

On many occasions I have witnessed individuals have similar experiences in the presence of Edwige. As owner of "The Spirit Within U," a metaphysical/Spiritual gift shop in Las Vegas NV, I've met many Spirits both seen and unseen., Rev. Dr. Edwige Bingue is a beautiful self-expression of God, peace, light and love.

KAREN MARIE CAMPBELL, OWNER, THE SPIRIT WITHIN U, N. LAS VEGAS, NV

"Since I started saying the prayers I started feeling my Higher-Self come through, talking with me. Amazingly, I now act with conscious awareness. Manifesting has grown better and my days are much smoother. After taking the protocol I went through a deep insight and awareness. I discovered I love my Higher-Self more than anything else as it's always there loving and listening to me. It's judge-less, beautiful and omnipresent. We can't see it with our five senses but we feel it on a level of knowing that. Even at times when we fearful, afraid of letting go and going with uncertainty, it's still there. Because of you, Edwige, I talk and feel with my Higher-Self on a much deeper level. The insights and help you brought me are phenomenal. Thank you very much. With love,"

JERRY GONZALEZ, STUDENT, CALIFORNIA

"Thank you for the class, "Raising your Consciousness." It was wonderful learning from such a smart, sweet, kind and nurturing person. I feel so blessed to know you and since we met, I feel like I'm growing through this intense process. The teachers that have come along have been amazing and I realize now more than ever, it's an inside job. Having the support from you has helped greatly. I see my progress and am grateful to my teachers. I am one step closer to being the person I've envisioned for so long.

The lonely journey has been incredibly challenging, but something in me keeps going and wanting to be the best me through the dark forest. Now I understand why you do what you do, Once again, thank you for being there and showing me your tools and techniques I can utilize in my pro-gression. There is plenty more to work past with my fears, and resistance to change, but I am one step closer. I know it in my gut. Thank you for believing me in me. Much love,"

JERRY SCHWARTZ, PRINT SHOP OWNER, PENNSYLVANIA

"I felt comfortable with Edwige right away. She has a calm that provides acceptance, love and she's easy to open up with. After talking with her, I realize my dreams have meaning. The touch that awakens me in the middle of the night and the voice whispering my name is real. I'm not crazy. I'm unafraid. I've started meditating and writing again. Fear of failure held me back in the past. Thanks to Edwige I realize it's impossible for me to fail at something I was meant to do."

BIANCA S. MITCHELL, PALM COAST, FLORIDA

Dedication

This book is dedicated to Prime Creator, the source of all.
The light that fills my being.
To every person on their path to enlightenment.
May your journey lead you to your soul's purpose,
and may you find the joy that makes your heart sing.
To my husband, Don House, who grounds me,
all while giving me wings to fly.
And to my mom, Marjorie
who inspires me to live each day in love.

Contents

Foreword

By Lava Bai

We are on this earth for a reason. We can either spend a lifetime trying to learn how to determine what life is all about or, we can simplify our lives and get to the business of living life with intention and clarity. "You're Not Crazy, You're Awakening" will propel you through the dirge of doubts, to a panacea of purpose.

Whether you are a Spiritual scholar or Spiritual student; seeker, lightworker or illuminary, this book is a quick read, filled with insights, inspirations and Spiritual truth. The exercises are a bonus and quite stimulating. The journal of encounters will intrigue anyone that has questioned, "Are we alone?" or "Is there anyone out there?"

For years, I went about life questioning my purpose. As the answers continued to unfold, I met Rev. Edwige. She is an amazingly gifted woman who has been blessed with the gift of Spiritual connectivity from a much higher level than most. In my lifetime, I have only encountered a few people with this gift. Her ability to intuit messages, intentions, and to align Spiritual imbalances is unquestionably divinely guided. How she managed to condense these techniques into book-form can only be attributed to the same Source.

In this book, you will have the benefit of experiencing two predominate voices of transformation: The first, the fluid, loving and supportively sentient, Rev. Dr. Edwige, and the other, the voice of her connected Self, who is able to rise into lucid, trance states. Throughout this book, you will have no doubt that Rev. Edwige is clearly advanced in her ability to connect with other dimensional planes. Regardless of her heightened gifts, she shares her experiences in ways that everyone can comprehend to the point where each reader can clearly master the techniques for their own respective Spiritual journey with ease.

This book will change your perspective about every aspect of your life. Rev. Edwige provides clear, simple techniques to expand your vision of life and how you are going about it. After reading this book and putting her easy methods into regular practice, it is inevitable that your life will change. Your consciousness will be transformed. You will become very clear about your purpose; and you will do it with ease and grace. And best of all, you will know that you were never crazy, because you *will* be awakened.

Preface

Awakening is a word that has become mainstream. Yet, it is not truly understood. While pondering this idea, I ask myself, "Why am I writing a book?" Quite honestly, writing a book was never my dream. I recall an encounter I had at a Spiritual workshop, where I was approached by a gifted Physic, and she asked, "Are you writing yet?"

I thought, "What are you talking about? You must be picking up on someone else's energy." I let it go until it happened three more times. That was before the experiences, as I call them, began happening about five years ago. I am finally in alignment with telling my story. In so doing, I hope to take you on a journey of discovering who you truly are, not just the physical you, but the real you. The you who has a soul purpose and a reason for being. The you who asks, "Am I crazy? Am I imagining the voices I'm hearing?" Or, the urging, *"There's something I'm supposed to do, but I don't know what."* If this describes you, read on. There is more at the core. Together we will discover it.

Allow me to take you on a journey, remembering you are a Divine Being having a physical experience. In this sacred space you will reveal to yourself what your script looks like. Are you living the life of your dreams? Or, are you on autopilot, doing the same things over and over, wondering why you're having the same results? I am here to tell you; today you get to start all over. Join me in a journey to self-discovery. A journey to consciously living your life with ease and joy, embracing the idea that life doesn't have to be, "By the sweat of your brow," to prosper.

My story of awakening began when my Spirit started trying to get out and break free. I felt like it was speaking to me, saying, *"When will you wake up and feel the vastness of all I am. I want to connect with you."* And, *"You aren't alone."* I started sensing this, but I didn't know what any of it meant. I had no idea where to begin. Was I making this up? Was I in fact hearing things from my Higher-Self? What is your Higher-Self?

I had no clue, and I could not find anyone out there having experiences like mine. What I knew was for that spark of light to pierce through the veil, I had to first learn to navigate the road to enlightenment. That is what this book is all about:

- How to recognize the guidance when it comes
- What it means to raise your consciousness and why it matters.
- What it means to live in your heart
- How you can begin to live a full and aware life.

Step-by-step you will be guided into creating mastery of your life and your results. Whether you want to improve a certain facet of your life, like finding your Spiritual Purpose, achieving a joyful and abundant life. I will help you unravel your feelings, needs, and wants, and. how to get unstuck so you begin manifesting the life you want.

This book is not only for those just starting on their spiritual path but for everyone on the path. My story is one of not only inspiration, or about my altered state of consciousness experiences, but it's also a journey of self-discovery, the realization of personal freedom, sovereignty, independence from limiting belief systems that kept us separate from our divine authentic self, and the attainment of our multidimensional reality realized. It is also about understanding how the inner workings of your mind, body, and soul work, so you have your own experience. The choice is yours; in fact it is your birth right.

Have you found yourself thinking you would never have chosen your current circumstances? Do you wonder how you arrived at the place you are currently in? How often have you pondered escaping your current life situation, diving into a life path that's more authentically "you?" We each have chosen our own journey. For many, this notion alone is difficult to comprehend and believe. But it is true. Whether a conscious choice, or an unconscious one, we choose our circumstances. If you desire to create change in your life, or completely change the direction your life is going, the choice is yours. The power is completely in your hands, or better, your consciousness.

As you read, I will reveal personal experiences which have impacted my life journey in significant ways and contributed to my growth. Some of these events may seem bizarre – even outlandish; some were painful. But, they happened. I now understand my conscious contribution to every aspect of these events, and how they led me to share with you. We each have an assignment on this planet. Are you ready to open yourself to your unique and special destiny?

You may think you never would choose your current circumstances or situation in a million years, but you did. The purpose of that choice was to cause you to expand in your own unique way. As you continue reading, prepare to expand both your mind and your circumstances.

Introduction

"Each person comes into this world with a specific destiny—he has something to fulfill, some message has to be delivered, some work to be completed. You are not here accidentally—you are here meaningfully. There is a purpose behind you. The whole intends to do something through you."

~~ OSHO

Chapter One

You Are Much More Than You Know

"You cannot transcend what you do not know. To go beyond yourself, you must know yourself."

~~ SRI NISARGADATTA MAHARAJ

LIFE CAN APPEAR LIKE IT IS GOING ONE direction, and before you know it, a massive shift happens. Suddenly your life moves in a completely different direction. There are always subtle signs that a shift is happening. The key is paying attention to the signs. Early in my life, I was given such a sign. At the time, I was unsure how to process the event. As I share my own experience, you may recall similar events that have occurred in your own life. Keep a record of whatever thoughts come to mind. Your notes will be invaluable later in helping you to connect the dots and awaken .

The Early Years

Growing up in New Jersey I thought my life was normal. Honestly, it was anything but normal. My parents built a home in the middle of nowhere down in South Jersey. I attended Catholic school, and dreamed of becoming a singer. Waking up in the middle of the night, I found the Spirit of a lady wearing a long skirt, a peasant blouse and a wide-brimmed hat standing in our lit hallway. This was a normal occurrence. There were times when everyone was downstairs and we heard the sounds of things moving around upstairs. Little did I know how much more would come.

Looking back I was never frightened of seeing ghosts, in fact I thought it was pretty cool. I often described them to my Mom the next day. Once, the Spirit of my great- great- grandfather appeared, He was looking in on me. Now I know and understand as we do the work to release karma, negative patterns, false programming, emotional blocks and more, it is released for our ancestors as well.

In the Bible in the book of Exodus 20:5 the writer says, "The sins of our Fathers are carried to the third and fourth generation" refers to this, genetically through the blood line (DNA). Our habits, illness and even personality traits carried on from one generation to the next. We have the ability to heal ourselves and our family line, for both the past and future. Then it happened, I was twelve when my first benevolent extraterrestrial being showed up.

Leaving My Body

One night as I slept peacefully, I felt the presence of something or someone in my bedroom watching from the foot of my bed. I opened my eyes, and there he was, a Spirit towering eight feet tall. A giant, at least from the standpoint of a petite eighty-pound twelve year old girl. He was pale, almost transparent, with small ears set high on each side of his face. His nose was small, barely noticeable, and he wore a long white robe. He was never intimidating to me. In fact he was quite loving. We communicated telepathically and I never feared for my safety or my life. I knew I was safe.

This was when I learned how to leave my body. I'll never forget the first time I saw myself lying in bed sleeping. At the same time I was hovering above my body thinking, *"How am I doing that?"* I remember floating down our hallway into my parent's room, seeing my Mom asleep. I tried to wake her, but she did not cooperate. Off I went out her bedroom window into the night sky. I discovered myself flying amongst the stars, looking out at creation. Then I would land on a bridge, and dive into the ocean depths.

These visits continued for six years. During this time I had two reoccurring dreams. The first, was a global event happening. My family knew to gather up in our upstairs bathroom, and I would guide everyone to safety. Everyone climbed into a large basket, suspended outside the bathroom window. The same kind of basket attached to a hot air balloon. I would climb out to the front, grab onto the basket and fly my family members to safety. The next dream was of everyone getting into a car, together we would drive down a long bridge to safety.

I've come to know Spirit was showing me I was a bridge between Heaven and Earth a vessel of sorts. I had no idea what this meant, but I came to understand years later.

Life continued unfolding with little change, until my Dad died one month before my nineteenth birthday. I felt lost and abandoned even though Mom was there. I had always been Daddy's little girl, now what? What doesn't kill you makes you stronger. That is exactly what I became; stronger. Shortly after my nineteenth birthday I became a blackjack dealer in Atlantic City New Jersey to take care of my Mom and my Sister. Until that time Mom did not work outside the home. During the three years I held that job, something always seemed "off." I never felt it was the right place for me, but I did not know why. Life has a funny way of happening whether you are paying attention or not. Life continued uneventfully until one day when I was twenty-five.

Once again, I was awakened to the familiar feeling of a Spirit watching me. It was that same benevolent being; this time he held what looked like a clip board. When I asked why, he communicated that he was checking on my progress.

At the time I still did not get it. I didn't comprehend there was something else I was supposed to do; I was just living life. Then the big move to "Sin City" (Las Vegas) happened. Or was it "Sin" City? I moved to Vegas in 1989. Life offered its share of contrasts, but for the most part I settled into my new environment well. As I pursued my aspiration to become a singer, I began auditioning for everything. I landed many jobs along the way. I also dated, but never made a true soul connection. I bought my first home as a single woman. Looking back, during my longest running gig, which lasted three years, my husband-to-be came to see the show many times. I was not tuned in, tapped in or turned on so we continued missing each other.

After that gig ended and I was playing at another casino, a girlfriend of mine, Tina called and told me she found my husband.

Tina was right. We fell in love and were married in 2002. Of course nothing you truly want in life happens until you become a vibrational match to it.

The Law of Vibration

Vibration is one of the many Universal laws governing everything we do. Understand we humans, and everything around us is energy, you must match the energy of what you desire. If I am a vibrational match to the idea and outpicturing of lack, then lack is what I will continue to manifest. That's where the old saying, "Fake it, till you make it," comes in. Personally, I prefer, "Practice the future" because I'm not into "fakery." The ideas is, instead of thinking and focusing on what you do not have, see yourself as already having it because your subconscious mind cannot tell the difference.

You are what you believe yourself to be as expressed in this verse from Proverbs 23:7, "As a man thinketh in his heart, so is he." Do we truly understand the power of our thoughts and the power of how those thoughts become cumulative? Our thoughts have an impact on us in either a positive or a negative way. Your thoughts are like a broadcasting station, sending out vibrations of what you think and feel. Then the experiences and the people you're a match to are returned to you.

Positive thinking does not mean keeping your head in the sand while ignoring life's less pleasant circumstances. Positive thinking means approaching the unpleasantness in a more positive, productive way. You think and believe the best will happen, not the worst. Positive thinking often starts with self-talk. Self-talk is the endless stream of unspoken thoughts running through your head every moment of every day. These automatic, uncensored thoughts can be positive or negative. Some self-talk comes from logic and reason. Other self-talk rises from misconceptions we create due to lack of information. I call this false programming.

A positive attitude stems from seeing things from our inner knowing, and, believing all is moving you towards something better. Therefore the power of positive thinking is directly connected to your ability to remove, control or eliminate negative thoughts. I have learned to both monitor my thoughts and develop a way of thinking positively so I no longer experience the unwanted things in my future as I've had in my past.

One tool I'd like to suggest is what to do when negative thoughts occur. The negative voice is something we all have and at times struggle with. You can take control of the nattering nabobs of negativity. When you do your positive attitude will shine through creating the life you deserve.

First, if you have a negative message come through; tell yourself, "Cancel thought. Cancel thought. Cancel thought." Or, "Delete, delete, delete." Replace the negative thought with a positive one. You can say the words to yourself. For example, if your negative voice says, "I can't do this, it's too hard," instead think, "Cancel thought, cancel thought, cancel thought."

Follow up with a positive affirmation like, "Nothing is too hard for me when I put my mind to it. In fact, I can do anything!"

At the moment you may be thinking, "This is silly." Or, "That won't work for me." Consider this, you did not get here overnight, so it will take practice and effort to reprogram yourself and chase away the negative thoughts replacing them with positive ones. Remember, it takes time and practice to develop a new habit. You may be thinking this is crazy or futile, however your persistence will pay off. Before you know it, not only will this new way of handling negative thoughts become automatic for you, but your negative thoughts will diminish greatly.

Ask, "What More is There?"

Settling into my new life as a wife, a business manager and a singer, was both joyful and extreme. My husband trains professional fighters, and, at the time we owned a boxing gym which I helped him run. We also owned several rental homes. At the same time I continued singing at different casinos when time allowed. Although I was busy and happy, I still found myself asking, "*What more is there to life?*"

For years I read all Spiritual books, periodicals and websites. I knew life on the other side was real, and we could connect. I just didn't know how to make it happen.

One day in 2004 while happily married and still living my dream as a singer, my life shifted in a highly, unexpected way. Contrast can have a peculiar way of bringing us into alignment with self. Better stated, contrast can aid us in connecting ourselves with our Higher-Self. When I say "contrast" I'm referring to those little bumps of unpleasantness which happen in life when you are not doing what you came to do. A startling event will take place to shake you up, wake you up, and get you on your path if you heed its wisdom. This event was about to take hold of me in unimagined ways, causing everything, everything in my life to change dramatically.

I was on the freeway en route to a photo shoot to promote my band. As life would have it I was rear-ended by a police officer driving about one-hundred miles per hour. You have heard people say that your life will pass before your eyes? It didn't happen for me. Instead I found myself in a still, calm, place. Perhaps I was in limbo just hovering and being quiet. Then what I guess was a second impact caused me to return to my body. I found myself grasping the steering wheel with every ounce of strength I possessed. I looked over to my Mom, my passenger. Her seat fell back. I asked her why she had the seat completely reclined. I did not know the seat could do that. She looked at me and said, "Sweetheart, we were in a car accident." I had no recollection of the impact from behind with the speeding police car.

Two weeks later I had my first encounter. "Experience" is actually the word I used to describe my visits from beings who came from other dimensions;

whether they were Extraterrestrials, Angels, Guides or Spirits. I also use the word "experiences" to include my travels to other dimensions, worlds, and visions that occurred both in altered and awake states of consciousness.

It is Finally Time

One thousand or more people gathered and, one by one, they were plucked up into the sky. I said aloud, *"Why am I not being taken up to the heavens? I'm a good person."* I heard a crystal clear voice tell me it was finally time to do the work I was sent forth to do. That work was to bring people into the light.

Okay, but what do I do? How do I bring people into the light? I thought. I began meditating, not very well at first, or even every day. But at least I started getting still and listening. A friend gave me a "Law of Attraction" CD by Ester & Jerry Hicks. Don, my husband listened to it first. He came to me and said, *"Are you ready for this? According to this CD, you brought the accident to yourself".*

I replied, *"Really, tell me more."* So my journey of what "this thing called life" is about truly began for me. Of course, I still didn't know what any of this meant, but I would soon.

That's when the urging began. I started feeling there was something I should be doing, but I was clueless what it could be. Still, I felt something within me changing, shifting. I started becoming aware in my dream state; I could rewind the dream if I didn't like the outcome. Or, while dreaming, I became aware of what was on television, even when my husband got up to get a snack. This keen sense of developing my multidimensional self, continued for months.

My dreams started becoming vividly real; as if I existed in two different worlds at times. My friend Karen a Shaman, who is like a spiritual doctor, offered to do a journey on me. A Shaman is a person who has access to and influence of benevolent and malevolent Spirits in the world. Shamans typically enter into a trance state during a ritual. They practice divination and healing. Not knowing what to expect, I accepted her offer.

She instructed me to lie down. Next she proceeded to play a drum she brought with her. Instantly I knew I was seeing colors swirling about in my vision. I also saw a pair of eagle eyes looking at me. When she finished we sat up. She told me at one time I was a Lemurian priestess who at one time led the lost land of Lemuria located between the Indian and Pacific Oceans. Part of my soul, known as a soul-fragment, was still there. This can happen when something traumatic transpires and causes your soul or your Spirit to fragment away and stay behind.

Imagine how many fragments of you are out there. They must be returned to your present body for healing to further your path. She saw me packing. As I did, I kept walking to the edge of the water, watching it rise. She told me I survived the sinking of Lemuria. In fact I saved several people, making it to Lake Titicaca in Peru. A fragment of me was still in that lost land carrying the guilt of not saving more people. Until this point I frequently tried to convince people they needed to wake up. I even tried telling them what they should believe. When the Priestess stepped back in I immediately realized I can only speak my truth. It is up to your free will to accept it or not. I finally found peace.

You Will Discover Your Truth

Everyone will come to their own truth in their own time and way. It is not our job as light workers to say how or when it should happen. We must hold the light, stand in our truth and shine as an example or a beacon of love.

Karen was also instructed by one of her guides in the Upper World, a world in non-ordinary reality. Or, the non-physical, a place primarily where Spirit teachers live. It is reached by going into a meditative or altered state.

She was told to show me how to visit my safe place where they wanted to teach me. A safe place is a secured sanctuary, reached from an altered state of consciousness. Once I knew how to get there, life became fascinating.

I would simply hear a bell ring; it could be the ring of a phone or the doorbell. Typically it happened at four-thirteen in the morning. The sound of the bell was my queue to wake-up and go to my safe place. The first time I went I had no idea what to expect. It was beautiful just like the secret garden you create it any way you choose. I was greeted by a middle age man, wearing an off-white pant set. He told me his name was Peter. Of course I had to ask, they don't openly volunteer information in that world.

From this place he sent me out to explore. Mostly I visited places and past lives. It was all so crazy. I would be in my safe place watching this scene play out on a big screen. I was in it, and, when it finished, the screen would go black and I'd be back in my safe place. Peter explained what just happened and why.

Other times there was no screen to watch, the experience was more hands-on, like when I found myself in what appeared to be a garage. A myriad of new tools were in boxes lying on the floor, and, there was a wall of cubicles. I started taking tools out of the boxes and placed them one by one into each cubicle. When all the tools were placed, with the blink of an eye, I was back in my safe place. Again, Peter was telling me I had all the tools, now it was time to use them. In another of my experiences, I found myself in a small room, ten by ten feet, in size ornately furnished with antiques. That room led to another and another with no doorways. All the rooms were furnished similarly with antiques.

I remember saying, "We should bring the walls down, there would be more room." The message I received was from the Bible, "In my Father's house are many mansions," from John 14:2. Then, "The walls are all coming down."

Next, I was in a room or perhaps a hallway with hundreds, maybe thousands of beautiful, silken sheets of fabric. They looked like chiffon, in rich jewel shades of browns, peaches and creams. As I continued walking, they gently billowed over my face, as if the veils were being lifted. Finally, I came to a standstill.

A tall, benevolent, female being stood nearby. She appeared seven to eight feet in height, maybe taller. I was not clear about her race at that time, but I came to know she was from the planet Sirius. She told me telepathically they were ready to teach me. I needed to meditate. You don't have to tell me twice. A few weeks later a friend and customer came to my store, (I owned and operated an Alkaline water-wellness store). She told me about a beautiful crystal she came across, called the Merkaba. She was so enthused about how wonderful it was and asked me if I wanted to buy one. I wasn't interested, so I politely said, "No."

Three weeks later I received an e-mail from another girlfriend. She went on to tell me about a workshop coming to town and they needed a home to host it. She said it was called, "The Flower of Life" and they were teaching the Merkaba activation/meditation.

Of course I was beginning to grow accustomed to synchronicities happening all around me. This was no exception. I hosted the three-day workshop at my home and once again experienced another shift.

Following the signs is so important. I explain it as if I'm on the Yellow Brick Road, and all I do is just take a step, the Universe does the rest. Not so. It goes without saying, but I will anyway. I started meditating every day. As I did, I began a Pandora's Box of visions from past lives. I was even gifted with seeing how, as the high priestess, I healed people in Lemuria, the lost land.

They showed me standing in my store and a woman walked in. She told me she was sick and would I please heal her? I replied, "Yes."

Suddenly I was standing in a cavern with chest deep water. The walls of the cavern shimmered with tiny mosaic tiles. Next, I noticed dolphins swimming around me, their vibration resonating through the water. Then the lady appeared in my arms again. I began swaying to the vibration of the dolphins and together she was healed. Being called to my safe place lasted a year, then Peter was gone.

Everything happens in cycles and Peter was there as long as it took me to get what I needed from him. I gained confidence in myself, knowing what I was seeing was real. I gained confidence in the process, allowing myself to go with the flow knowing as I needed it whatever I needed in the moment would come to me.

The way may not be clear for you at first, but with practice, patience, and perseverance your way will become crystal clear over time.

Chapter Two

Preparing To Connect To
What Is Beyond

"The real voyage of discovery consists not
in seeking new landscapes, but in having
new eyes."

~~ MARCEL PROUST

✳ ✳ ✳ ✳

AS YOU GAIN CONFIDENCE IN YOUR PERSONAL PROCESS of growth and expansion, you will also begin mastering techniques to attain and maintain greater clarity. The first steps in this process are developing the skills with which to connect. You will also discover how to get off living on autopilot and start the process of breaking free and becoming your authentic self. As you begin attuning yourself to the connection of higher vibrations, your awakening will develop. During my own growth and expansion, I started getting visits from a plethora of different beings.

Experiencing Visitations

One night, while my husband was en route to California, I was awakened by a warm embrace. There was no one else in the house but me. When I finally opened my eyes and looked to the left of the room I noticed a beautiful golden, lavender orb leaving.

In the moment, I was aware I was experiencing an angelic visitation. I knew I was beginning to raise my vibration enough for them to see me, and thus, allow me to actually see them.

In my public speaking appearances, attendees often question what is required to experience these visits. My answer is always the same: Raise your consciousness which raises your vibration, then the real you is revealed. Then, you can let go of the baggage and the things which no longer serve you. When you do that, the chakra just above your head, the eighth chakra, better known as your Christ consciousness, turns on. Then the cosmos can see you.

Remember, if you are energy and energy vibrates, you must vibrate at a higher frequency; a frequency beyond the third dimension.

There are other things you can do to release and increase your vibrational level, like decalcifying your pineal gland. What is a Pineal gland and why is it important? It is part of the endocrine system, and, it produces serotonin a derivative of melatonin, a hormone affecting the modulation of waking and sleeping patterns. Its shape resembles a tiny pine cone and it is located near the center of the brain, between the two hemispheres. Our lifestyle habits over the years can create calcification or hardening which can prevent release and higher consciousness. On the physical level it has been known to contribute to Alzheimer's disease. Decalcifying the pineal gland can create an opening for the third eye. Decalcifying can be as simple as putting a tablespoon of apple cider vinegar, or lemon juice in a glass of water and drinking it daily.

Spiritual speaking, the Pineal gland is regarded as a "Spiritual antenna", the mystical third eye ancient traditions discuss. For eons, the third eye has been seen as a way to reach higher levels of consciousness while remaining present in our physical bodies. Thus, if the pineal is your "Spiritual gateway to all realms and dimensions" it is important to make certain it is fully functioning. Before reaching this Spiritual gateway, you must start the practice of detoxifying and activating your pineal gland, through changes in diet, and, Spiritual practices including meditation and visualization.

As I look back at the car accident (my contrast experience), my desire to recover in a natural way facilitated the decalcifying of my pineal gland and my awakening. Remember, you must be willing to let go. Which becomes easier as your consciousness elevates.

The key is to remain open, unafraid and willing to expand. Expect the unexpected, knowing as you awaken, becoming more consciously aware, raising your vibration, your team and all those light beings standing by to assist will start showing up.

At times I would be touched in the middle of the night, or, the bed would shake in an attempt to gain my attention. As I mentioned before, this stuff is not for the meek of heart. I saw colors every time I closed my eyes. I was told I was seeing my team of entities, teachers, and guides assigned to me. There are quite a few of them, about six to ten guides at any given time. A new one showed up recently, a male energy. He glows a brilliant green, unlike any shade of green in this dimension. I also have a blue, a violet-white and magenta energetic guides.

Members of the Team

When I discovered these were members of my team, they celebrated doing what they do; making spirals or shapes, like concentric circles or strobing lights. They have not given permission to share their names, but I can tell you: one guide has been with me since the beginning of my incarnations. It is a female energy. Another holds my blueprint for this lifetime, and is also a feminine energy. My relationship guide is male in energy. Finally I have a humanities guide, who is masculine in energy, too.

Shortly afterward, I saw a dazzling white light in the distance. The brightest light I have ever witnessed. As it approached I opened my eyes to make sure I was indeed seeing it. Yes, I was. When it got right in front of me, it became like the toy ViewMaster I had as a child. Still shots of pictures began appearing in my vision with my eyes both opened, and closed. I saw silly, colorful cartoon characters, one after the next, each lasting twenty to thirty seconds.

My understanding is I was being prepared for what they would teach me. This was a tune-up session. It was essential to remember what I saw, and, I knew I had the power to see and grasp whether my eyes were actually open or shut. Since this encounter I came to discover the reason I am experiencing these things physically is because this is exactly what I asked for before coming into this time-space existence, this life.

At that time strangers gave me messages of love. I could be out and about, just doing day-to-day activities, and without fail, a person would approach me saying, "They want me to tell you how much you're loved." Or, they would say I am, "Supposed to be writing my story." I was attracted to attend several Spiritual workshops, mostly in Sedona, Arizona, a center for vortexes and Spiritual activity. I studied Theta Healing, and was guided to enroll in the University of Metaphysics. This is where I received my Masters and Doctorate of Metaphysical Science credentials. My body and mind became highly attuned to energy and energy fields. A sense of deep knowing started filling me, and, I was finally ready to begin sharing what I knew. These experiences became part of the work I will share with you in this book.

In 2011 I started hosting an internet radio show called, "Affirmations for Living." Each week thousands of listeners join our upbeat discussions as we look deeper into Spiritually-based principles. My listeners discover it is their birthright to live with passion, purpose and prosperity. It's a weekly opportunity for both me and my listeners to connect to our true authentic selves, and become aware of our higher self.

I am in demand for one-on-one transformational coaching and healing sessions. I also hold webinars designed to get my students away from living life on autopilot and thinking more consciously. I conduct workshops and am sought after for speaking engagements. I have a guided mediation CD which I sell online and in local stores. I am a frequent guest at Holistic, Spiritual and Health expos and fairs where I often provide free mini counseling sessions and hands-on healings. I do energy healings, activations and am a vessel for Source or God energy.

Many of the people I work with experience immediate healings. Others experience a removal of emotional blockages which have kept them stuck for years. As you read in the paragraphs above my gift was spontaneously activated. I did not consciously seek it out, but where I was led I followed. I look a bit like the people you see on television who start speaking in tongues when Spirit takes over. Yes, I am aware it seems kind of crazy to many people, but the flow of Source energy is very strong for me. Whatever the person I am helping needs most in that moment is facilitated through me.

Why I Wrote this Book

I wrote this book because I am constantly asked questions by my listeners, students and clients. It was time to finally go more in depth about my story of awakening and the solutions to what may be troubling you. I am so excited you are reading this book right now. I was provided and experienced answers to help you understand what happens when you begin awakening and expanding. Awakening your consciousness is an amazing journey, and, when people begin to notice shifts and changes they ask questions. Below are some of the most frequent questions I hear and I will address in this book:

- What is consciousness?
- How do I move beyond feeling and being stuck?
- Why do I keep sabotaging myself?
- Why work on clearing emotional issues, if my karma, or destiny, is set anyway?
- How can I manifest more of what I want?
- How do I figure out what's blocking me and holding me back?
- I didn't choose this. Why are so many negative things happening to me?
- How do I know what my soul purpose is?

As my chakras began activating, I started heating up. My feet began vibrating more each day. Then, the vibrational sensations began moving up my body, and I felt energy in my center or core. Next it moved to my hands and so on, until gradually my entire body was pulsating and vibrating on an almost continual basis. These experiences intensified as time went on. One morning I was in a light sleep state. I woke up and saw a brilliant, ultra-violet bright light coming toward me, once again. It didn't matter if my eyes were open or closed. Even with my eyes closed its brilliance seemed to pierce through my eyelids. I saw it growing closer. As it did it began taking the shape of an eye or a cone-shaped pineal gland. What looked like electrical currents began pulsing around it. The energy grew stronger and more intense to the point I felt it in my eyes and my head.

Then my body began vibrating. I saw the current increasing in potency to the point it reached critical mass and burst in my eyes. I shut my eyes immediately and tightly thinking they may be damaged, but when I opened them they were fine. I felt the incredible expansion of knowingness it created all over.

When I opened my eyes instead of seeing each color as separate, I saw a mass of changing colors like a beautiful kaleidoscope with all the colors of my team violet, blue, magenta, and green swirling together. Not only was my frequency amplified, but my pineal gland was fully activated. During this time I was directed to prepare my physical body for even more expansion. Then my team of guides told me to stop eating meat.

How you accept and apply the information coming from your benevolent beings is something you must decide for yourself. Understand as you raise your vibration, it's best to consume only what is a vibrational match like food that is still alive and the purest of water. I was drinking pure alkaline water and avoiding fluoride, and chlorine, which in the opinion of me and many others blocks the awakening process, by calcifying or hardening your pineal gland as discussed earlier in this chapter.

Your Health and Awakening

What is lurking in our environment can have a big effect on your awakening and expansion. I've already discussed the pineal gland and the importance of eating live, healthy foods. Dare I mention chemtrails?

Chemtrails are the remains of ongoing atmospheric spraying of arsenic, aerosol, aluminum, barium, depleted uranium and substantial amounts of mercury. When you see white trails of what looks like steam or engine exhaust at the back of a high-flying jet, those are chemtrails. Geo-engineering experts claim the spraying arrests the effects of global warming. There's only one problem, what goes up, must come down. These chemicals are seriously polluting our air, waterways and soil while seeping into crops and contaminating livestock. They are also changing the weather patterns. Plants are especially sensitive to the soil degradation that occurs with chemtrail spraying, creating serious issues concerning our food supply. Anything that chemically alters our bodies impacts our health and our ability to grow and expand consciously.

During the days chemtrails are most visible I wear a mask to drive. I am not paranoid, but we certainly live on a three dimensional planet, so we must act accordingly.

The more I awakened in consciousness, the more experiences happened when I was in non-altered states such as sleeping. The gift is when you are awake and can see you are in a better place to consider what the significance of these "visits" is for you.

It was three in the morning when I felt my body being pushed into a wall. Like when closing a dresser drawer. The sudden movement jarred me awake. In my vision I saw the colors of my team swirling rapidly. A spiritual download was coming and they were getting my attention. I was lying on my side, but I felt like I was lying on my back.

My head began vibrating and pulsating. My feet, hands, and core started intensely vibrating. The colors and energy in my head grew more powerful, lasting several minutes. I was told I was gaining access to records and timelines. When the experience finished, I looked at the clock beside my bed. It was 3:33 AM in the morning. Numbers have significant meanings, and, this sequence, "333" represents the ascended masters.

The next day in meditation, I called upon Jesus, my younger half-brother in Biblical times. Joseph was a widower, and had a daughter Ruth, I was she. Then he married Mary. I have a vague recollection of myself and Jesus at a well as we gathered water together. The colors I normally see this time formed the shape of a heart. I felt the presence of my beloved brother, and stayed in a place of grace and love.

Desire and be Open

We are never alone and our team of Spirit guides wants to connect with us. But, we must ask for their assistance because this is a free will planet. Nothing is ever forced upon us, even when it's for our own good. I was discovering the awakening process is a hands-on one. It's not enough to merely say you want to wake up, and, "Poof!" there you are. It is a process, with many steps. Only through perseverance, compassion, and sincerity will you traverse the journey with sanity. It truly is like peeling back the layers of an onion, allowing for more of your authentic self to shine through. However when peeling back yet another layer, many have said, "Darn, that onion gets big sometimes." Desire is the first step, of course. Earlier I mentioned you must raise your consciousness. But how do you do that?

Meditate for Peace and Awareness

Meditation was the second step of awakening for me as told to me by a Christed Extraterrestrial being from the planet, Sirius. A daily practice of meditation has worked for me. In getting still, God can connect with you, and then begin revealing self as self. As a spiritual practice, meditation is a conscious act of participation in being. Create a meditation or prayer practice for yourself and watch the results. Whatever it looks like for you, just get started and do it.

For the beginner who has never meditated before, or, if you do not have a clear routine, here are a few helpful ideas. Use what speaks to you as appropriate for you.

There are many ways to meditate. Your practice may include prayer, an invocation, a visualization, concentration, and/or perhaps contemplation. As a spiritual practice, meditation is a conscious act of participation in being. The importance of getting still is expressed in the Bible. In Philippians (4:8) the writer says, "...finally, brethren, whatever things are true, whatever things are noble, whatever things are just, whatever things are pure, whatever things are lovely, whatever things are of good report, if there is any virtue and if there is anything praiseworthy; meditate on these things."

Meditation requires a degree of self-control for the physical, emotional, and mental bodies. For me the object of meditation is living in higher consciousness consistently, while also working through my lower instrument, the physical mind and body.

I like sitting upright in the yoga position, remembering to keep my spine straight, and taking a few deep, long breaths, relaxing further with each breath. Then you:

- Set your intention to connect to God. Call to God silently or aloud.

- Ask the energy of Divine Will to fill your entire being and to reveal to you whatever you want to embrace, shift or manifest.
- My suggestion is asking for personal power, strength and will to begin.
- Connect to Spirit and spend time in the stillness.
- You may choose going into an affirmative or visualization segment of your meditation. For example, envision good health, a new job, love, and joy.
- Focus on God's presence at a point half-way between your eyebrows. This is where your third-eye chakra is located, and, the top of your head, where your crown chakra is located.
- Allow the energy of the third eye and your crown chakras to come together in a pulsing power of will.
- Relax and let the power of God's Divine Will, flood your conscious and subconscious mind, thus adding your desire to align with God's Will and giving you power over your subconscious desire.
- Imagine your third-eye has the ability to breathe, just as if it's your nose. Then relax into the in-breath, the out-breath, and the space in between.
- Focus your attention on feeling the energy of will, strength, power, purpose, and whatever gifts you desire. As they flood your being, know they will merge with your will and God's will, too.
- Stay in this space as long as you like, giving attention to every cell of your being.
- Allow it to flow freely from your Higher-Self and your conscious awareness into your subconscious mind.
- When you are ready to come out of the meditation.
- Thank God for his/her assistance, and begin following the natural flow of your breath again, opening your eyes when you are ready.

Of course you must find what works for you, but this gives you a sense of what meditation is like. Awakening is about uncovering who you truly are.

Begin Trusting in Yourself

I'll never forget once when I intended to make a stop at Wal-Mart® before going to the Alkaline Water Wellness Store I owned and operated. I got in the correct lane to turn left into the store parking lot when I heard a voice loud and clear inside my head say, *"Turn right!"* I wondered why. After all, I need to get to the store. Again the voice said, *"Turn right and go home."*

At this point I started talking to this voice saying, "I'm half way between home and my store. Why can't I just go to the store, I'm in the lane to turn left?"

The voice said, *"No one is behind you, make a right turn and go home."*

"OK, fine," I said, made the turn and went home. I pulled into my garage, parked, and took the few items I purchased inside. When I returned to my car and sat in it to run another errand, it would not start. I had it towed to the auto mechanic shop from the comfort of my garage. I said a big "thank you" to my team for their persistence in telling me to go home. Thanks also to me for finally listening, too.

While this may appear to be a small thing, dealing with a stalled car in the Las Vegas summer, desert heat would have been an inconvenience that day. I am grateful for the persistent message from my team of guides that helped me arrive home safely where I could deal with the situation from home rather than stranded in a parking lot.

- Are you tuned in to the small messages that come your way daily?
- Do you appreciate the value of developing your conscious listening skills?

You might ask, "Edwige, how do I do that? I would love communicating with my Spirit guides, too!"

That's why raising your consciousness, thus your vibrational level is so important. You'll begin opening the channels to your Higher-Self and other dimensions. The voice will come in different ways. You may get flashes of pictures, or scenes in your inner vision or outer vision. You may hear the voice from within. For me, I also hear an outside voice. It may come as a gut feeling or a knowing. I was told because my vibration is so high; it's easier for my team to communicate through the language of light. As they shared, words cannot fully express what they are communicating in the higher dimensions.

As part of my agreement coming forth into this time-space reality as "Edwige" I knew I would be born with fourth dimensional consciousness and vibrate high enough to have these experiences, awake and aware. The key is becoming aware of your language, and, being open when your team communicates. So, listen to how they communicate.

A practice I teach my clients is setting an alarm clock to wake you up between four and five AM in the morning. That's when you are in alpha brain wave state and more receptive and open to communications. Lay quietly asking your guides or teachers to tell you their name or anything you want to know. Then wait. Before you know it, a flood of insights, feelings, messages and visions will begin coming through to you.

Become a Conscious Thinker

Another aspect of raising your consciousness is becoming a conscious thinker. You have probably operated on autopilot the majority of your adult life. You:

- Do the same mundane things
- Work at the same job
- Eat the same food
- Hang out with the same friends and
- Generally keep the same routine.

You get the idea. In this place your subconscious gradually takes over and continues creating the same, repeated patterns in your life. The synapses in your brain or as I sometimes call them, "brain grooves" become more deeply entrenched in their ways of doing things. Consider this: Ninety percent of everything you do is based on what is programmed in your subconscious, whether you want it or not, even if you like it or not. Is it any wonder you keep having the same experiences? How do you wake up? Become conscious in your awareness, and begin giving conscious thought to every moment. What you think about today will manifest itself in your future. We become trapped by our beliefs and they hold us back.

Early one morning I found myself unable to breath. Something that felt like plastic, or a mask was over my head. I realized I wasn't in bed, but I was elevated, suspended vertically over my bed. When I looked down I saw my feet dangling in mid-air. I remained calm and serene considering what was happening.

My Higher-Self guided me and I knew to say, *"Whatever no longer serves my best and highest good, with all my love leave now."* I saw a bright green light, and suddenly the plastic or mask was off, I was back in my bed able to breathe again. Dramatic? Yes, I agree. But I know part of my soul purpose is remembering these experiences so I fully understand their meaning and can share them with you.

I was becoming my authentic self; the butterfly was finally breaking free of my cocoon. Layer by layer my truth was gradually being revealed.

Moment by moment my purpose was becoming crystal clear. I could see, feel and hear beings from higher-dimensions so I could share with you, my readers, they actually do exist. There indeed is something more and you are but a moment away from experiencing it yourself.

It is essential for you to become aware that you are creating your reality in each moment. If you are to shift into higher-conscious experiences then you should stop throughout your day, and ask yourself:

- What am I creating in this moment?"
- Is it serving my highest and best good?"
- Carefully evaluate what you are thinking, and
- How it makes you feel

If you like what is showing up in your experience, fine, then continue. But if you don't like what is showing up, stop. Ask yourself, "Why am I thinking these negative/dis-empowering thoughts? How can I cancel them and rephrase them in a more positive, empowering way?" Take responsibility for your life and acknowledge you are getting back what you put out. I know this may seem harsh to some readers. You may believe you would never choose your current circumstances or situation. But you did, and the purpose of your choice was to cause you to expand in your own unique way.

Release the concept of duality or polarity of thought, for a moment. Let go of the notion of right and wrong, good and bad, or, black and white. For that matter liberate yourself from the mistaken idea you were cast out of heaven and must work your way back. Instead, look from the perspective of the place I discussed earlier, when I was with two of my guides, writing the pages of this book. When you see the bigger picture, you will realize every experience is about moving you forward on the path of awakening.

It does not matter how it showed up in this illusionary world. You, as a divine, perfect, being will be just fine. Your team undoubtedly will assist you along the way. Keep in mind, you must connect with your team first, of course. The point is, stop beating yourself up and judging everything in your life from a place of disconnect and fear. Rather look at everything that occurs as the amazing, fascinating journey of discovery it is. Appreciate that every experience is serving you in one way or another. This is a spiritual journey, and it begins and ends with you.

What are you willing to do? Are you ready to:

- Stay the course to your personal awakening no matter what?
- Hold yourself accountable for your actions, thoughts and feelings?
- Love yourself unconditionally no matter what is revealed to you?

In the beginning as I had more frequent experiences, I started asking, "Why me?" Why was I seeing all these things and having crazy experiences? Early one morning the answer finally came to me.

It was about 4:00 AM in the morning. I found myself in another place, this time chanting "HU," an ancient name for God. This activated me into starting another type of chant, which caused my entire body to vibrate and move into a completely new zone or feeling. It moved me to another place. In this place I began bleeding from all over. I do not recall any pain, but I somehow knew the sins of my father were being removed. My lineage was being cleared for me, for my family in the past, and, for my future family. It was an amazing feeling. The blood represented the DNA, or, as the Bible says the sins of our fathers will be carried down three and four generations.

As stated earlier, your habits both good and bad, your personality traits, even your health conditions are carried from one generation to the next through your genes. As you do the work to release what no longer serves you, so you do it for your family as well.

Next, I was in a vast space, greeted by an enormous being of light, twenty or more feet in height, who said he was a gatekeeper. It became clear I was in the cosmos. Millions of twinkling stars glittered around me. Suddenly a tube-like vortex made from what looked like millions of overlapping leaves to create a tube, was suspended above my head into the highest reaches of the cosmos. If you can imagine, the vortex tube was in hues of purple, ultra violet, and magenta. I knew it was connected to my crown chakra because I felt it pulsating and vibrating. The being of light told me I had the key, and could bring in anything I wanted through this vortex. It was now open.

As I looked up into it, as far as the eye could see I noticed energy swirling with stars. As I focused on, love, the success of my soul purpose, and completing what I came forth to do, I also called in prosperity. At that moment, I felt a shift. I had a new, exciting sensation of strength and empowerment. The experience ended and once again I was back in the space of my room comfortably in bed.

I started my morning prayers. When I finished, I went into meditation. The powerful energy I felt looking into the vortex was still with me. I always go into my heart space during meditation and call in my team members. When I called them in one by one I knew exactly why they were with me. Our mission together, next to all the Christed extraterrestrial beings assisting me came in as well. They surrounded me and I felt their loving presence. I knew I was ready to fulfill my soul purpose and mission, I would receive whatever was needed, and I was more powerful than I could imagine.

Getting tuned in to you is an important part of the process of awakening. Meditating is a window into tuning in and part of the process, so let go and let God. Tune in to yourself and watch the amazing things that happen. You are opening a window for the Divine and the experiences your guides, your team want to bring you when you begin meditating daily.

Combine meditation with conscious, clear thinking and trust in yourself. You will gradually begin noticing amazing, positive changes.

Chapter Three

Letting Go Of The Gunk

"It is always the false that makes you suffer, the false desires and fears, the false values and ideas, the false relationships between people. Abandon the false and you are free of pain; truth makes happy, truth liberates."

~~ SRI NISARGADATTA MAHARAJ

* * * *

ONE MORNING I AWOKE TO AN IMAGE OF a torus in my vision. A bright purple, revolving circle with a red heart superimposed over it. The colors were brilliant. A tetrahedron appeared to the right of it. A tetrahedron is a geometrical shape with four triangular faces. The tetrahedron began spinning very fast. As it did, I began leaving my body, flying into the cosmos extremely fast. I was in space before I knew it. I was both frightened and calm, so I said, "In the name of Jesus bring me home." Once again I was comfortably and safely back in bed again.

I realized some of these experiences were happening a little too fast for my comfort. I needed more preparation time beforehand so I would not be afraid the next time an experience showed up. If you believe you are a divine spiritual being, having a physical experience as I do, you must know why you came forth to have these experiences, and how to handle them best. If you are reading this book and drawn to the message, I suggest you are a "Starseed. Starseeds are people who originate from far-distant star and solar systems, planets, and galaxies. As highly evolved souls, Starseeds carry an abundance of wisdom and exceptional abilities that hibernate deep within the core of their being. You are not just any Starseed but one who has come forth to give birth to the New Earth.

On this free will planet we call Earth, the evolution of man must be undertaken by man. That is exactly what we signed up to do. Lifetime after lifetime we incarnated to experience self, our Godself, except we forgot we are actual extensions of Source energy. So we began feeling separate and less than divine. We took on all sorts of dysfunctions, like fear, guilt, shame, poverty, lack and every limitation you can imagine, and made it our own. In fact we grew highly effective at believing these limiting ideals were our truth, and we were less than perfect and divine.

Within our DNA is coding. At the absolute ideal time we begin awakening, which causes us to start asking questions. Important questions like, "Who am I?" You may have started feeling changes in your beingness taking place, and, a sense of urgency regarding the, "What now?" questions. The significance of the "what now" questions are about beginning the process of regaining your divinity. Your true divinity is part of the collective consciousness creating an evolution in humanity.

As a Starseed, as a Lightworker, and as answers to the "Who am I?" and the "What now?" questions are revealed to you, your contributions are pivotal in the evolution of the new and improved human being.

It seems like a daunting task, and, when you think about it, yes, it is indeed intimidating. You may be asking yourself, "How can I possibly think of myself as divine when I know my dysfunctions. How can I consider my divinity when I have been living this life, mighty convincingly I might add, as less than light and far from a perfect human being?" This is exactly why you must start seeing and acknowledging your own divinity.

The assignment you accepted is transforming all the lower vibrational, dysfunction you previously embraced whole-heartedly. False programming must be addressed and released to support you in stepping into your Higher-Self, and, becoming the co-creator you are. As you do the work to release your old gunk, the new and improved you, the you who has released lack and limitation of every kind will emerge. That emergence will catapult us into the future. The future is here now.

With the birth of the New Age came a plethora of modalities available for the releasing of these dysfunctions. I discussed meditation earlier. Now, I will discuss other methods I believe are effective, and I have been guided to share with you.

The Power of Visualization

Let us take a closer look at the power of visualization. Visualization is defined as a technique which includes focusing on a positive mental image to achieve a specific goal or objective. The practice of visualizing will help you shift your thoughts and create what you desire. What you want in your physical world first must be created in your subconscious before adding your energy so it can be realized. This makes visualization a critically important tool to master. You must give the correct orders to your subconscious mind; those thoughts and images which control and govern all your experiences. Here are seven keys to visualize what you want to create:

- First your mind cannot tell the difference between what you imagine and what you perceive as real.
- Adjust your thoughts and focus your attention on the scene you desire until you completely identify with the picture.
- Go into a light meditative state. Fill your mind with a picture of the results you desire for your life.
- Imagine a goal you have in mind, and play it through like a movie, ending with the result you want to experience.
- Hold this feeling for a moment. Then come out of the light meditation, knowing you can easily invoke the feelings again at will.
- Finally repeat the mental picture or movie until it becomes your new belief.
- Personally, I combine a transcendental meditation and connect to all that is.

After you have done this as long as you choose you can go into a visualization segment similar to the one already discussed. This time, as it plays out in your inner vision, you send white light to surround the ideal picture or scene. Then, send it love, holding the space for a moment while saying, "It is done." Ideally, visualization should be done in an environment that cultivates an atmosphere of quiet and relaxation. My meditation room suits this purpose. With candles and incense burning I can easily relax. I enjoy playing soft, instrumental music which elevates my consciousness and opens my heart. From this space, I easily enter a light meditative or quiet state. This means I quiet myself mentally, physically and emotionally.

Affirm the Best of Your Intentions

Now I will review the use of affirmations. As you know my weekly internet radio show is called, "Affirmations for Living" so it should be no surprise to discover I consider affirmations a highly useful tool. I find them most useful filling the space created after releasing the old gunk. If you do not fill the space, the old stuff may return. My experience is, writing affirmations for yourself is beneficial. It allows your new, positive thoughts to be set into action. Following are some principles I believe are vital to the success of using affirmations to increase your consciousness level.

First, create your affirmations in a positive way, using the present tense, as if what you want has already manifested. Be short, succinct and specific. An example of this is, "I am now confident and successful." Next, call up the feeling, or emotion which is a match to your desire. Doing so, your subconscious is more apt to believe it. Also, begin your affirmations with "I am." The "I am" is a recognition of God and our Godself. Here are more examples of affirmations:

- I am abundant, prosperous and enjoy my success.
- I am healthy, whole and complete now.
- I am a divine being having a human experience.
- I am loving, kind, caring and worthy of love.
- I am joyful and grateful for all my blessings.

- I am excited and enthusiastic about the day.
- I am a perfect example of God's love working in my life

The best time to recite your affirmations is first thing in the morning as you wake up. Remember, you are still in the alpha brain wave state when the subconscious is most open to new suggestions. Another good time for affirmations is when you retire for the evening, and you are in the theta brain wave state. Again, you are more receptive to new suggestions and ideas. There is no set length of time for affirmations to be effective; it depends how deeply-rooted your negative beliefs are that you wish to transform. Next, repeat, repeat, and repeat the new affirmations again and again. This helps reinforce the new belief and thought pattern. Finally, believe the process works. Even if your natural scepticism causes you doubt, choose to believe it anyway. Once your subconscious is gradually programmed to believe the new affirmation, the brand-new belief converts into positive action for your conscious mind.

There are many more ways you can shift your thinking such as the Emotional Freedom Technique, known as EFT. This is a form of psychological acupressure for the emotions, based on the same thirteen energy meridians found criss-crossing vertically and horizontally on the body, which are used in traditional acupuncture. Acupuncture, originally developed in China, has been used successfully to treat physical and emotional ailments for over five thousand years. The advantage of EFT? It can be as highly effective as acupuncture without the invasive use of needles.

The process involves a simple tapping on various parts of the upper body with the fingertips. This inputs kinetic energy onto specific meridians located on the head and chest while you contemplate your specific problem whether it is a traumatic event, an addiction, pain or something else. This process occurs as you voice positive affirmations aloud. The combination of tapping the energy meridians and saying positive affirmations works to clear the short-circuit or emotional block from your body's bio-energy system, and restore your mind-body balance.

The Inner Voice Appeal

Self-Hypnosis is an artificial way of self-inducing an altered state of consciousness. In this state, suggestibility and receptivity to directions is heightened. The technique is used to implant goals or ideas into your subconscious mind. The easiest way to do it is to make a tape recording of things you desire, or the beliefs you would like to change. Listen to it when you retire for the evening. Just as with affirmations, the statements should be short, positive, worded in the first person, and stated as if the goal or desire has already been attained. If you can, loop the recording so it plays for a full hour or more each night while your subconscious is open to receiving suggestions.

Another tool I have embraced with good results is the Violet Flame. The Violet Flame comes from both Father-Mother God. It is intended to help humanity transform into the perfection of light the human miscreations we mistakenly manifest through our negative thoughts and feelings. The Violet Flame is a balance of the out-breath of our Father-God, represented by the sapphire blue flame of divine will, power and authority. The in-breath of our Mother-God is represented by the crystalline pink flame of transfiguring divine love, compassion, adoration and a reverence for life.

When the two merge, a violet flame is created. It has the ability to change into light every mis-creation we have experienced. Because we live on a free will planet, you must invite the Violet Flame into you through an invocation. This includes calling in your guides or teachers, asking for their assistance. You invite the Violet Flame in by invoking it through your "I AM" presence. Again, the I AM presence is considered by many as our

Godself or God-energy. It enters from above through a silver cord to your crown chakra. Then it descends into your heart flame. When the Violet Fire enters your heart flame, it is stamped with your individual electronic pattern awaiting directions.

Each person has a unique tone or frequency, which is how your karma finds you. It emanates forth from your Heart Flame, stamped with your personal electronic pattern or frequency. It travels through the atmosphere of the earth at atomic and sub-atomic levels and then expands out into the Universe. As it does, it seeks and magnetizes to itself every electron of energy vibrating with the frequency of the previous false belief. It activates the new potential, vibrating to the original frequency of perfection.

This doesn't happen overnight. It is based on you reaching critical mass which means fifty-one percent of the energy, vibration and consciousness of whatever you are shifting has been achieved. When fifty-one percent of your energy at an atomic and sub-atomic level is now vibrating to a new higher frequency, the remaining forty-nine percent will instantly be absorbed into the vibration of your new belief.

We never know when this will happen, so you must be patient and keep invoking the Violet Flame until the change has manifested in your physical reality. Following is an invocation I use: "I AM my beloved. I AM presence invoking the full power of the Violet Flame to transmute the cause, to transform the core effect record, and, the memory of every thought, word, feeling, or action I've ever expressed in any time frame or dimension, both known and unknown, that reflects (fill in the blank) poverty, poverty consciousness, fear, guilt, or lack and limitation of any kind."

Certainly you can customize the invocation for your individual use. Only you know what is holding you back. Many people find this empowering when you are able to vocalize and invoke what you are transforming to the Universe.

As mentioned earlier, when you clear the false programming of old, you are left with a void or space. That void must be filled with the new vision or dream you hold for yourself. In addition to visualization and positive affirmations; if you want to recreate yourself, you must begin painting a picture of your recreation.

I have a worksheet I use in my classes and workshops. Attendees answer questions about, "How do you see the new you when it comes to your health, relationships, finances, career and spirituality?" It is time to consciously create what these changes look like for you. See yourself as you wish to become and write them out. As you start becoming aware, you become a witness to what you want to be, do and have. When you pay your bills bless them, give donations and state your gift will return to you one thousand fold. When you see a loving relationship between two people like you want to manifest say, "That's great. I admire them and I am expecting a loving relationship of my own soon."

Change Your Thought Process

Do you see how changing your thought process greatly impacts your experiences?

Dare I say another wonderful practice I have embraced is going into silence. Yes, getting quiet. There are so many external feeds and white noise bombarding us every day, this is especially so in the internet age. We have become over-stimulated which can slow down our increasing conscious awareness. How can you possibly expect to hear from your Higher-Self through all the chatter and chaos? In order to hear your all-important inner voice, and the guidance we each have within us you must periodically turn down the external stimuli. This means shut off the television, the internet, the phone and all electronic interruptions for a few hours each day, allowing you to tune in and listen to your inner voice. Before going to bed, take a moment to check in with yourself. Bring to mind your day's events:

- What does the day look like for you?
- Was everything resolved one way or the other?
- Or was anything left unfinished?

The amazing thing about connecting is you receive so many opportunities to grow and expand. For example, if you find as you review your day, something feels unresolved, ask your Higher-Self to move toward a resolution as you sleep. If you have a new project or something you wish to pursue ask your Higher-Self to show you the process while you sleep. Of course, remember it.

When you tune back in, make a conscious choice to fill the space with positive, uplifting inspirations and motivations that bring joy and lightness. This is because the Universe works in accordance with being positive. If you understand everything going into you programs you one way or another, I know you would rather be programmed with good, positive ideas and not negative ones you will need to work through, right?

You must first understand how your subconscious mind, or, the memory banks of your mind work to create lasting changes. The relationship between the conscious mind and the subconscious mind is like an onion. The conscious is represented by the outer skin of the onion which is easily viewed. In contrast, the subconscious is represented by the hidden, soft, fleshy interior. The subconscious mind works according to the Law of Belief which states; you can have anything you want if you release the belief you can't have it, as long as what you want does not conflict with another's beliefs.

In Mark (11:23) the writer says:

"Whosoever shall say unto this mountain, be thou removed, and be thou cast into the sea; and shall not doubt in his heart, but shall believe those things which he saith shall come to pass; he shall have whatsoever he saith."

The subconscious is the largest part of your mind. It holds all the messages you have received throughout your existence and learned through repetition. Then it groups those messages into beliefs, habits, mindsets, and character traits. Those messages determine:

- How you feel
- Whether you have a positive attitude
- Or a negative attitude.
- And they determine your success in life

From this point forward your subconscious is in control of your footsteps and, how you will perceive new experiences. This is fine, if everything in your life is satisfactory and going as you want. But how do you move from a place of un-winning to winning?

This is why you must be a guardian of everything entering your mind. Everything you see, hear and feel goes directly into your subconscious. This means managing the information you allow in, and, eliminating negative information like negative news and violent movies, as much as possible. I make a daily practice of using positive words to reinforce the attributes I desire. For example, the words "can't," "don't," and "try" are low vibrational words. Using words like this magnetizes you to low vibrations and low energy that will bring you down.

Be a Guardian of what Enters Your Mind

"Capable," "will" and "achieve" are higher vibrational words magnetizing a higher energy to them. Lower vibration words are heavier and cause a lower feeling to stay with you longer. In contrast higher words are fleeting and require our constant attention. As you move into the process of reprogramming your subconscious, pay attention to your new vocabulary to experience lasting change. Therefore, everything you find in your physical world is created by you first, in the inner world of your mind, either consciously or unconsciously. Also, because your thoughts are energy, you must take care of the direction you send them. For example, if you are worried or anxious, your thoughts and energies will magnetize toward the reason for your worries.

Perhaps you worry about your finances. Your thoughts direct your energies towards the source, the reason for your financial problems. Focus on this, and according to the Universal Law of Attraction, you will attract more negative things. This is not good. Knowledge of the interaction between your conscious and subconscious mind will enable you to transform your whole life. To change external conditions, you must change the cause, which is internal in nature. Most people try to change conditions and circumstances by working within the framework of those conditions and circumstances. To remove discord, confusion, lack, and limitation, however, you must remove the cause of the condition. The cause is the way you use your conscious mind; in other words, the way you are thinking and picturing in your mind.

I have used all the techniques mentioned here at one time or another with remarkable results. I am confident as you embrace these ideas, you too will make lasting changes in how you communicate with your inner self. As we make use of these processes it is important to remember how our breath plays into every one of them.

Our breath is critically important. Within our breath is the life force, "prana" as it is known in Sanskrit. Most people are shallow breathers, or chest breathers drawing minimal air into the lungs, usually by drawing air into the chest using the intercostal muscles rather than throughout the lungs via the diaphragm. People who take shallow breaths do so throughout the day. Most are unaware of the condition. This cycle of poor breathing, can cause tension and low energy, which makes raising your vibration difficult. Deep pranic breathing leads to our bodies releasing stress hormones. When you are tense or stressed, you hold your breath or breathe in a more shallow, irregular way. This leads to greater tension, more stress hormones in the bloodstream, and in time, an establishment of the fight-or-flight response as your normal condition.

You did not start out this way; in fact, shallow or chest breathing is learned behaviour. Every baby instinctively breathes from the abdomen. You can see this watching small children and babies as they sleep. It took me one week of practicing pranic breathing every day while meditating to get accustomed to it.

The steps are straightforward, but like everything new, be patient with yourself. You can close your eyes, or, keep them open through this exercise, whichever is more comfortable for you. If you're doing pranic breathing during meditation, you will probably close your eyes. Here is the method to do it:

- Sit on the edge of a chair, sofa, or bed, whichever you choose.
- Keep your back straight and away from the back of the chair or sofa
- Place both thumbs on your navel and spread your hands across your lower belly. This gets you used to how you feel when you expand your diaphragm.
- Place your tongue on the roof of your mouth behind the hard palate, the hard ridge behind your top row of teeth. Keep it there while breathing. This connects two major meridians, or energy channels, enabling the flow of prana. One meridian runs down the front of the body from the palate to the perineum. This is the "conception" or "main" meridian. The other runs from the perineum up the spine, over the back of the head, down the forehead, and ends at the top of the palate. This is the "governor" meridian.

- Exhale through your mouth until your lungs are empty, but do not strain. Your stomach should move in, but try to keep your spine straight.
- Begin breathing in slowly through your nose.
- Feel your lungs filling up in three segments: first the abdomen, then the ribcage, and finally, your chest.
- Your chest should not move as you breathe in, only your abdomen.
- As your lungs reach capacity, pause for a moment. Then exhale smoothly and gently through your nose.
- This completes one cycle of pranic breathing.
- Continue working on your stamina adding seconds each time you practice. Go gently with yourself and in time you will amaze yourself with how much better you feel just by breathing the way nature intended.

Remember no matter what the world says you are a Divine being. You are good enough just being yourself.

Chapter Four

Protecting Yourself

"One evening an old Cherokee told his grandson about a battle that goes on inside people. He said, 'My son, the battle is between two wolves inside us all. One is Evil. It is anger, envy, jealousy, sorrow, regret, greed, arrogance, pity, guilt, resentment, inferiority, lies, false pride, superiority, and ego. The other is good. It is joy, peace, love, hope, serenity, humility, kindness, benevolence, empathy, generosity, truth, compassion and faith.' The grandson thought about it for a minute and then asked his grandfather, "Which wolf wins?" The old Cherokee simply replied, "The one you feed."

~~ UNKNOWN

I T WAS ONE-THIRTY IN THE MORNING WHEN I noticed a green serpent in my vision, and then it came into my room. I paused briefly, thinking was I seeing things. Before I knew it, the serpent was consuming my right arm, swallowing it. This was not good, and, I stayed fairly calm considering the experience. I said, "In the name of Jesus, I command you to leave." It paused momentarily which was unacceptable. Energetically I moved my left hand. I hit it and commanded it, saying, "Now!" and the serpent disappeared.

It's amazing how, when dealing with our energetic self, our I AM presence, our Godself takes over. We are calm, confident and know exactly what to do. This leads us to a discussion about grounding and protection. Once again I say we are spiritual beings having a physical experience. This means we are more energy than we can imagine. We must learn how to work, energetically speaking, with all aspects of our multidimensional self.

The Danger of Awakening too Quickly

Why must you ground yourself? While traveling your path of awakening and increasing your consciousness and vibrational level, you will experience a variety of things, even symptoms. Some events and feelings can be easily explained through conventional terms, others not so much. What people do not tell you is most of these symptoms can be reduced or eliminated through easy techniques.

When I started awakening years ago so many things happened. Back then there was no list of symptoms or good resources available to help. I remember my Shaman friend, Karen, saying things like, "Be careful. You seem to be awakening too quickly." She even hinted dark forces might be at play. What she and others did not realize is what took her and many of her generation two decades or more to attain, took me four years.

What has taken those I counsel two years to gain, may take you the reader one year or less, because this is the time we all have been waiting for. As we move out of linear time, we move away from the old standards, and old ways of doing things. We get to make up the rules as we go along, and, we have the Universe supporting us.

I remember another visit, the anniversary of my Dad's birthday; September 15th. He would have been eighty-nine years old. I went to bed the night before thinking of him as I do every mid-September. In the middle of the night I felt a being enter the room. I did not recognize him, but as he began speaking I knew it was my Father. He told me he loved me. I was thrilled to know I could actually communicate with the other side.

Send Some Souls Home

I fell back asleep and in the wee hours of the morning, was awakened by a crystal skull. It came in from the right side stopping in front of my face. It was greenish in color and light came from its forehead or third eye. At first I was excited, talking a mile a minute; until it said, "Shut up!" That was my cue all was not well. I quieted for a moment and listened. It went on about needing my help, and then had the nerve to ask if it could implant something in me. Without hesitation I said, "Hell no," and it left.

As previously discussed, as you awaken and raise your vibration, what is known as your eighth chakra turns on like a light. The cosmos and all its inhabitants, both good and not so good can see it. That is why it is so important to ground and protect yourself every day

Astral Travel and Grounding

Now that your eighth or crown chakra is open, you may be able to astral travel, or, feel you are leaving your body. Ground yourself so you do not feel spacey and unbalanced.

What exactly is grounding or earthing? The obvious idea is having one's feet on solid ground and/or walking with certainty. It also means being fully present both physically and spiritually in this dimension. The latter part can be quite challenging. I know it sometimes still is a task for me. I can start a spiritual conversation and feel myself drifting out of my body. It even happens when I am teaching my, "You're not Crazy" classes. Knowing I am a multidimensional being, able to leave my body at will can be daunting at first. So learning the techniques here is incredibly valuable, especially on those nights where we all would appreciate uninterrupted sleep. Grounding is also beneficial to help you feel balanced, increase your inner strength, your self-confidence and your focus. It helps your spiritual development providing an outlet and allowing the release of energy more easily.

Grounding and Protecting Yourself

Grounding should become a part of your daily routine. With time it will become second nature. Consider first some of the most common symptoms of being ungrounded. This list is not all inclusive, but it will give you a strong indication of what it means to be ungrounded You will discover yourself experiencing the same one or two symptoms each time you become ungrounded. The symptoms include:

- Dizziness and/or feeling spacey
- Day dreaming or falling asleep while praying/meditating
- The opposite of falling asleep, insomnia.
- Difficulty focusing or forgetfulness
- Feeling sick, heart palpitations,

- Eyes flickering, weight gain
- Inability to manifest good ideas
-

For amateurs, I suggest first setting your intention, and, second clearing your energy with sound and visualization. There are few easy techniques I use to help me ground myself. The first, called "Rooting Yourself," uses visualization. Try this:

- Imagine your root chakra, located at the base of your spine, is glowing red.
- Now see it beginning to grow strong, sturdy roots like a tree.
- Let the roots go down into the earth and let them anchor you to the earth
- See and feel the roots expanding, connecting you to Mother Earth.

Rooting yourself is a quick technique to help you get grounded. The next technique is even easier. We use crystals, which are easy to carry, and have incredible power. Always clean your crystals with sea salt and distilled water. Set your intention for this purpose before using crystals. Any small piece of tumbled stone is sufficient to carry with you. Here is a partial list of the easier crystals to work with:

- Red jasper (most jaspers are effective as grounders)
- Bloodstone
- Hematite
- Gold Tiger's Eye
- Carnelian
- Garnet
- Pyrite
- Copper

- Amber and
- Unakite

When I feel myself beginning to float away I grab my red jasper and hold it in my hands, it works like a charm. Finally, go outdoors and hug a tree. Or, remove your shoes and stand on Mother Earth. When I do, I feel energy rushing down into the earth, like bands that have connected us and she is pulling my hands and feet into her. Depending on your personal circumstances, you may want to seek the support of a spiritual practitioner, a respected Shaman or even a professional therapist who specializes in spirituality. Seek professional care if you feel you need it. Far better to err on the side of caution.

Another morning I was lying in bed between four and five AM, when my body began pulsating and vibrating. The colors became vigorously active in my vision. My head felt like it was being squeezed, almost like a vice grip on my head. Then, images began appearing in my vision. Images I saw with my eyes open or closed. These images were coming in quickly, every one, to three seconds. I saw the ocean, what looked like Aztec or ancient Egyptian symbols, and medley of different images. At one point I asked them to ease up on the intensity because my head was actually hurting. I came to discover they were not attempting to give me knowledge, they were aiming to retrieve knowledge I hold. This brought up the question of, "Who am I that they would know I had certain information of value?"

The answer came two years later, when a guest on my weekly internet radio show did a clearing session with me. I called him after the show to thank him for being my guest, as I do most weeks. He asked, "Is there anything you want to know or have cleared?" I thought and then asked him, "Who was I that these beings knew I had information to save their race?" Pretty deep stuff, I know. In the Chapter five I will share what was revealed in that session.

Seeing as You Awaken

Another time, an energy shoved the bed which woke me up. This time I asked, "What do you look like? I want to see you." All the brilliant colors swirling in my inner vision got still. Then an opening appeared in the center of the swirling colors void of any color or movement. I intuitively knew to look into the void. When I did, I saw into another dimension. I was looking at these beings, but they did not notice me because they were walking with their backs to me. Shortly afterward, it appeared one noticed I was looking in on them. It came to the edge of the portal or opening, and, for a moment we were looking face-to-face. This being was pale blue, hairless, with large golden eyes, and, had textured skin, like a lizard. Yes, a reptilian. We gazed at each other for a moment and then the portal closed.

As the experience continued, a piece of paper materialized in my vision. It had a meditation on it. The meditation told me to bring in the four directions. I was trying to read and understand it, when they shook the bed again. This threw me off guard and I fell back in bed. The next time I saw the pale blue, reptilian being was a few weeks later. Early in the morning my body started pulsating and vibrating. The colors started a feverishly dance. Without asking the portal appeared.

Again I looked in; this time I saw a room about ten by ten feet in size. The room was changing colors. But the colors went from the bottom of the wall to the top. The room was being "painted" two shades of purple or ultraviolet. The blue, reptilian beings appeared again with their backs to me. This time they looked busy as if they were diligently preparing for an important arrival.

I felt the bed covers lift off me. Slowly, inch by inch, all the covers were removed. I wasn't scared, I was curious. When the covers were completely off, I began levitating. I felt myself lift off and move past the bed. I laid suspended for what felt like ten minutes when my entire body began pulsating and vibrating at an extremely intense rate. It was more intense than I experienced before. Afterward, I returned to bed not truly knowing what exactly happened. That was the last I saw of them, but I never forgot them, and how they helped facilitate my awakening.

Since that experience, I came to discern like people, there are good and not so good beings. Thank God, the race of blue, reptilian beings who contacted me were at least half-way good. They needed information to save their dying race, and, I held it.

Once again my Shaman friend, Karen, did a journey with me. I was not surprised when it was revealed I had a reptilian attachment. That was the easiest way for them to obtain information. Karen removed the attachment. As she did, her teacher in the upper-world said they did not harm me; in fact they did some good. As far as I was concerned it was time for them to go. This brings me to the next point: protection. Let me share what an "attachment" is and how it works. There are two basic types of attachments:

- The first are Spirit attachments, non-physical energetic beings which attach to your aura, the human energy field. These Spirit attachments are human souls who have died and not yet crossed over, or, gone to the light. Because they have not crossed over they are stuck here on earth as either whole souls or parts of souls. They attach to humans to continue life on earth, living off the energy from humans. They can maintain a type of control and power over humans. Most people with these attachments never know it. They live out their entire lives with these attached entities.

- Another type of attachment is a dark force attachment or entity, and, a non-human dark energy. Dark force energy is negative and fear-based. These beings are tasked, or sent to this planet, with the intent of causing harm, misery, pain, and stealing the energy and power away from humans.

Dark forces, as their names suggest, are a darker, more negative form of energy than Spirits. They cause deeper, more serious issues in the people to whom they attach. Both dark forces and Spirits cause a host of problems mostly related to emotional, mental and energy-level issues. Both these kind of attachments fasten themselves to people through cuts and holes in the energy field, your aura.

Your aura is an invisible layer of electromagnetic energy around your body, which encompasses your physical, emotional, mental and spiritual bodies. Auras emanate from every person just beyond your physical sensory perception. Next is a simple practice to train yourself to see auras if you choose:

- Find a suitable background. For example if you are looking at the aura around your hand, a large sheet of white paper works well. When viewing the aura of a friend, it is important to have them sit or stand in front of a plain wall.
- Proper Lighting: Lighting should be not too bright or too dark. Natural light like sunlight or a candle flame in a shaded room is best.
- Position yourself or your friend: If reading your own aura, hold one hand against a white background in any way you are comfortable. If reading another person's aura, have them sit or stand comfortably in front of a white background. Their clothing should be solid in color, or, be void of too many patterns.
- Relax your eyes as you gaze at your subject. You can look at your fingertips, or the head of the other person.

- Now, let your eyes gradually unfocus. You should begin seeing a haze around the edges. It may appear bright or cloudy.
- Determine any visible colors. You may see one dominant color or several colors.
- Be aware of "after images." If you stare at the same spot too long, your eyes will begin seeing after images, which are not auras. Focus directly in front of your eyes for a brief moment and then try again.
- Be patient. When you first notice an aura, be persistent. It may disappear as soon as you blink or shift your eyes. It takes practice to hold your eyes steady.

Mental, Emotional and Spiritual Bodies

The Mental Body is the energy field which holds your core beliefs about yourself, others, and the Universe. It assists in processing information, solving problems, and generating higher abstracts thought.

The Emotional Body is the center of your feelings and emotions. For example: Love and hate, attraction and repulsion. When used with the mind, it provides desire and imagination. It is also the location for sensual enjoyment. The most interesting thing about the emotional body is, when you sleep, astral perceptions are picked up as dreams. The emotional body holds all memories and experiences you have encountered.

The Spiritual Body is your soul's link to the Universe. When this body is purified from limiting beliefs, false programming, and perceptions, you can more fully connect to Divine Will and unity consciousness. This body organizes and vitalizes the physical body. It acts as a bridge between all bodies, by way of your chakra centers and the meridian connections.

Your aura constantly exchanges energy with everything around it, unless you decide differently. Whether you are aware of it or not, everyone reacts to this subtle energy. These cuts or holes are created in your energy field from negative or weak emotions and a loss of personal power. Personal power can be lost through the use of drugs and alcohol, weakening your energy field. Soul loss can also weaken your energy field. Soul loss is caused from traumatic experiences, weak or negative emotions such as fear, anger, and depression. It also creates energetic openings which allow the entry of these Spirits and dark forces.

Spiritual protection is something everyone should know about, regardless of your religious or non-religious beliefs. Negativity in any form is damaging to the human energy field and aura. Even negative people, places, arguments and more can create negative energy which clings to you, or, builds up in your home, causing problems over time. There are signs which build up indicating you are indeed, unprotected. Symptoms can affect you on both an emotional and spiritual level.

For example, you may feel irritable, drained, defensive, have nightmares, be overly emotional, experience pain in your neck, your solar plexus and your back to name a few. Some of the easier ways to build up protection of your energy field are to maintain good health, eat live foods and drink the best water you can find. I drink alkaline water.

Wearing certain colors such as gold, silver, violet or blue can help. Carry crystals with protective qualities such as Amethyst, Lapis Lazuli, Gold Tiger's Eye and Hawk's Eye (blue tiger's eye) for psychic protection. Next is a simple visualization exercise you can do for your protection from entities, spirits and possible dark forces:

- First imagine you are sitting in an egg of light. The base of the egg is sitting just below the floor, allowing you to ground yourself.
- You are surrounded in your egg by a lovely protective color (gold, silver, violet or blue).
- Make sure your eggshell is solid. See it as between one-half an inch to two inches thick. This way no negative energy can penetrate.

- Any negative thoughts or emotions you have will not get out, and, no negative thoughts or emotions from others will be permitted in.
- Each negative energy or thought pattern will hit the eggshell and slide down it into the ground to be transmuted in to positive energy. Only the highest vibrational thoughts will be allowed inside.

In turn, check the outside of the shell for any rips or tears. If you find one, sew it or mend it with your thoughts or imagination, however you choose

Chapter Five

Putting Your Pieces Together

"Every act, thought and choice adds to the permanent mosaic: Our decisions ripple through the Universe of consciousness to affect the lives of all. Every act or decision made that supports life, supports all life, including our own."

~DAVID R. HAWKINS MD, PHD
TRUTH VS. FALSEHOOD, 2005

TWO VERY FAMILIAR EYES APPEARED TO ME, BECKONING me to come forward. Because they were eyes I was used to, I was comfortable enough energetically, and I felt myself move toward them. I noticed one of my power animals, a peacock, was with me. It was early morning again. Are you noticing a pattern of when these visitations typically occur?

I found myself in Africa, tribal Africa in fact, probably dating back hundreds of years. The setting seemed ancient, like a scene out of a movie. I felt my physical body and Spirit exist in two different bodies. As I observed everything I felt my Spirit in the body of an old woman. I saw my physical body on a platform, where they were about to perform a ritualistic sacrifice. I intuitively knew I had the power and the strength with my power animal to go on to the platform and demand my Spirit and body be returned to me. Through my simple intention and command it was done and I was back in bed.

I can now do my own soul retrievals. "What exactly is a soul retrieval?" you ask. A soul retrieval is the process of bringing back or retrieving part of your soul when it fragments or separates from you. A soul fragment is part of your wholeness disconnected and moved beyond the reach of your emotional resources and intellectual capacities.

Soul Loss and Retrieval

Soul loss, mentioned briefly in Chapter 4, can occur when you have a traumatic experience, be it physical, emotional or spiritual. If soul loss occurs from a trauma, a piece of your soul will choose to split from the whole and experience, feel, or, take on the trauma. At that point the fragmented part of your soul leaves this dimension, allowing the soul to continue without fully experiencing the original pain.

In ancient or tribal cultures, a Shaman retrieves your lost soul fragments going into a Shamanic or altered state. He or she uses animal energies that agree to help. Once all the fragmented parts are retrieved, she returns them to the person by blowing the fragments into their chest. This process is called a Soul Retrieval.

Some indicators to look for if you think you may have soul loss include:
- Any block or memory loss, particularly from childhood
- Depression of any kind
- Panic attacks of any kind
- An inability to separate emotionally from another person

Soul loss can express itself as strongly as deep depression, or, as lightly as a slight feeling of emptiness or a sense of disconnection from life. Often it shows up as a sense of internal limitation, or, a feeling you are struggling too hard in one particular area of your life. You may experience a sensation as if you keep reaching for something that keeps slipping away just out of your grasp.

Retrieving Lost Soul Fragments

My team of Spirit guides showed me, as a team we now have the ability to retrieve our own soul fragments. Of course if your Higher-Self is not guiding you through it just yet, you may want to try a guided soul retrieval meditation, or, do your own research to discover what works best for you.

My husband travels extensively as a cutman for the UFC, Ultimate Fighting Championship. Early in our marriage I experienced anxiety every time he left for work. I always attributed my fear to the fact my Dad made his transition and crossed over when I was only eighteen. The incident left me feeling abandoned. For years I believed I associated my husband's travels with the loss of my Dad. Let me add, my Dad was a chef on cruise ships and traveled extensively as well. This leads me to share a personal experience which helped clarify my previous feelings of loss.

I found myself in Italy. It appeared like old world Renaissance Italy. Once again, I was a woman. I noticed an older couple with the little boy walking towards me. They seemed familiar. When they reached me, I bent down to ask the little boy how he was doing. He told me he was okay, but somehow I was not convinced. I became extremely upset, distraught and began crying.

Instantly I knew the little boy's father was my fiancé who died shortly before we were supposed to marry. The older couple was my fiancé's parents. They brought the young boy, who would have been my step-son, to visit me, and, see how I was coping. Next, I heard a voice outside myself say my fiancée was in the light. It was time to release the emotions of loss and heal a deep wound and a previously lost soul fragment.

As I returned from my altered state, my team provided guidance. I knew I experienced a deep, sad loss in that life still impacting me in this life. It was not the death of my father that caused anxiety when my husband traveled; it was the loss of my beloved fiancé from another lifetime. My team said I didn't need to know the details of my fiancé's death, but let it go with positive intention, and that would be enough to heal that fragment.

As the multidimensional beings we are, we have all experienced many lifetimes both on and off planet Earth. Indeed, as divine beings having a human experience, we exist on many levels. Not just energetically speaking in our auras as discussed earlier, but also in parallel lives, past, present and future, all coming together in the here and now. As your awakening progresses, more of your fifth dimensional aspects are integrating into your physical body. While mastering the concept of being multidimensional you will gradually grasp this concept whole-heartedly.

Clearing and Clarifying Energy

Everything is energy whether you perceive it as human, animal or inanimate. If an experience or trauma was part of you in any time-space reality there stands a chance it could use some clearing. I stay in contact with many of the special guests I interview on my internet radio show. As I mentioned in Chapter 4, one particular guest specialized in clearing energy. We spoke after the show and he asked if I wanted to clear or clarify anything. I had an amazing experience of clearing an off-planet existence.

In the previous chapter, I stated I would explain why reptilians visited me for three months. Here is where the story continues: What information did I hold? How did they know I held the information they sought? As I sat in my office speaking with my radio show guest on the phone, I entered another dimension of consciousness.

I found myself off the planet as a priestess. There was a global war taking place and I was standing inside a temple helping people. There were many species there, unlike earth where there are only humans.

On the left side of me was a small girl afraid, bent over in fear. I saw myself, as a priestess, comforting her. Then I noticed on the right side a male reptilian being sitting down in a chair dominating the energy which caused the small girl to feel fear. He was blue, with textured skin, large amber-colored eyes and with no hair, just like the blue reptilian beings who came to me in this lifetime on this planet. The practitioner had me sit for a minute and hold or feel the energy of what was happening. Of course metaphorically speaking, both were different aspects of myself:

- The reptilian began letting go of his dominating energy.
- The little girl gradually discovered her power, releasing her fear.

As the girl released her fear she grew into a woman. In my vision, I saw the color pink to the left and noticed blue to the right. The colors began swirling in my vision and then came together. As they did, they merged and ascended.

The practitioner told me they were a part of one of my soul groups and were returning to Source. As we sat and took in the magnitude of what was happening, a magnificent blue color came into my vision. I began pulsating, vibrating and heating up as the energy of my soul opened, clearing each chakra to its full potential. I basked in the energy of it, as I saw my soul.

Next, I saw a scene of a field; gray in color, as we continued giving attention to the energies that needed healing. One was a Druid-type, ancient European, Celtic, male energy. He was influencing thousands of souls attached to him.

At first, he seemed to put up resistance, stomping his feet, not wanting to return home for fear of losing self into unity consciousness. I sat and said to myself, "I know even though I am one with unity consciousness, or God, I will maintain my identity." With that, he stopped resisting and was returned to Source.

Drinking in Life Force Energy

As more things were removed it appeared the scene came to life in full color. The canopy was revealed, and, all aspects of me at every level seemed to be clearing and returning to my soul. A golden version of me materialized, and then my life force came into view. This golden energy began flowing through me down to Mother Earth and through her core, connecting me to a crystalline grid. I felt it moving through me. A few times I opened my eyes because it felt like I was rocking in my chair. Mother Earth began drinking this life force.

I felt it come in as if someone turned on a faucet above my head. I sensed my entire body move throughout the process. I continued opening my eyes to look from time to time, because I experienced an incredible amount of movement. For example, my heart was pulsating so strongly, it was as if something was moving out of my back from between my shoulder blades. Mother Earth continued drinking the life force flowing through me. I was aware of it all the way down my feet. When it finally stopped, I noticed the earth had a new energy, looking brilliant and vivid in color. We waited several minutes, holding the space of love and gratitude for what just took place.

Suddenly, oozing black stuff was kicked off the earth like black gunk flying away. Some of it was the size of continents. Dark energy was finally being forced to vacate the earth. My practitioner told me, the Earth needed this. I held within me both Source power and Soul power. In all his experience, he told me he never encountered this combination of powers in another person. He told me I gave the Earth the life force needed, and, I hold special light codes, and creation templates. My aura was larger than Earth and nothing could touch me now. Amazing! Thank you GOD was all I could think.

The road to self-discovery can be fascinating. There are so many different aspects. You must open your mind to possibilities you may never have thought possible a year ago, for that matter even yesterday. But to discover your true self, you must at least consider these ideas and decide what is true for you.

To understand soul retrieval better, we need to consider how multidimensional we are. Many different religions and philosophies believe after physical death, the soul or Spirit begins a new life in a different body. This includes the idea you may return as either gender, or any race or color. We endure a series of lifetimes for the purpose of spiritual growth and soul development. We are all working towards the eventual escape from the cycle of birth, death and rebirth.

Past lives can impact us in many ways. Think of it like a classroom: you learn all manner of occupations, professions and vocations to experience greed, anger, selfishness and pride. After acquiring these selfish traits in the separate self you relinquish them to return back to interconnectedness.

That means you could have experienced lives not only in all types of jobs, but all nationalities, all sexes, including homosexual, and, you have experienced being the bad guy as well as the good one. With hundreds or thousands of incarnations to act out all these categories, you can begin letting go and transform yourself into a better soul. Your circumstances, talents and inclinations to a large extent are caused by your experiences from previous lives. They are based on how you lived that life.

You create what is known as your karma. Karma is a Sanskrit word meaning action. When we think, speak or act we initiate a force which reacts accordingly. Those deeds or energetic forces travel with us from lifetime to lifetime. What we have been in the past makes us what we are, good or bad. In this life, or, in a reincarnation. It becomes our starting point. What we do with that starting point, what we choose to change or keep, is our choice.

A Multidimensional Existence

Let me share the concept of being multidimensional, because it is an essential concept in your awakening process. All humans are multidimensional. In fact, all life on Earth is, including our beloved pets. The challenge is, somewhere along the way we forgot our natural or divine nature, which has caused a disconnect from other aspects of the self. This world exists right in front of you. The multidimensional self can be considered as a series of parallel realities blending together to form the Universe we call home.

Your perception can experience four dimensions within the physical plane: Three create space, the fourth creates time. Physics states there are more, but for the sake of simplicity we will stick to the basic four. These fields are electromagnetic in nature and change as they get further away from the body.

- Closest to the body is the etheric field
- Next is the astral field
- Third is the causal field and finally

Within the Astral and Causal fields or planes there are intermediate levels called spheres. Each of these spheres has the potential to develop into another complete realm. As we move away from the body the properties of the field become lighter in density, thus the name "subtle body." Another exciting point about this movement outward is as we move outward, and grow lighter in density we also increase in vibration. This means as we move from spiritual into physical, the spiritual state is at a higher vibration. As vibration increases, density is reduced.

The etheric field is composed of a substance called ether and can be easily seen by most people. The etheric is more energetic in nature than the astral or causal planes. It is an active element, involved in the functioning on the physical plane, and, the management of biological functions in living systems. Look at a person or object, and then gently unfocus your eyes. You will see a soft, shimmering light field, like an outline, just outside their body.

The astral plane has two major subsets:
- the emotional plane, and
- the lower mental plane.

The emotional plane governs our emotions. Most psychics tune into it easily. The lower plane governs the operation of the mind. Few have developed the ability to see the lower mental plane. Typically you see color and size variations as well as an intense illumination. When I do energy work on a client, I see color and movement based on what my Higher-Self is doing. When my Higher-Self is working on a heart wall or block, for example I will see green, but my heart will shake trying to break free. In fact I can feel it breaking free. Or, when someone is being healed, a white light will go to the injured area on the body. I never know what to expect. Even if a client comes in for one thing, but must be cleared, the clearing will occur first and foremost.

The casual plane also has two subsets:
- the upper mental plane and
- the spiritual plane

These are involved in our higher mental aspirations, and, our spiritual nature. This plane is very subtle and more difficult to see directly.

As multidimensional spiritual beings, not only do we have these planes of existence in our body, but these planes also exist when we are in the non-physical. There are many stories of people who physically die and come back to tell their stories of briefly crossing over. We are similar to icebergs; only a small portion of our being can be viewed from the surface. There is much more going on below. We are increasingly developing the skills to look deeper into what lies beneath the surface.

The energy signatures within the fields surrounding the physical body are traces of your subtle bodies, and, operate on other planes, too. The functioning of one subtle body is interdependent with the functioning of all other subtle bodies. This is why there is such emphasis and importance placed on the balancing of chakras, removing blocks, and clearing your energetic fields.

Choose to Remember and Connect

Do not worry if you cannot sense or see these fields, because you are forever in them. You, as a spiritual being, are the sum of all your bodies stretching across all planes and dimensions. The optimal functioning of your body and mind happens best when all the bodies in all the planes are working harmoniously as one. Managing a multidimensional reality is essential when you seek to evolve spiritually and improve the quality of your life. Being aware and connected to the multidimensional world is an innate truth. Losing the conscious connection to your multidimensional nature is like losing a sense; it has a profound impact on how effectively you operate, and, why you must consciously choose to remember and connect. All the interdimensional parts of your being work together in synchronistic harmony.

The more flexible your conscious mind is to witnessing the truths of your reality, the more effortlessly all the parts adjust into each other. When you hold rigid beliefs, your perception can become blocked, causing the parts to jam up and eventually creating stress. Just as you are following along, reading the pages of this book, you have also followed along is your path to greater consciousness and awareness.

This is a clear indication you are open to the concept of being multidimensional, in theory at least. So begin opening yourself to more possibilities, releasing the old programs. Release the false belief in duality; that you are separate from God. Release the belief you are a sinner who was cast out of heaven working your way back. Know and believe now, you are a divine being having a physical experience. Enjoy the ride.

Chapter Six

The Blocks Come Tumbling Down

"Our intentions – noticed or unnoticed, gross or subtle –
contribute either to our suffering or to our happiness.
Intentions are sometimes called seeds.
The garden you grow depends on the seeds you plant and water.
Long after a deed is done, the trace or momentum of the intention behind it
remains as a seed, conditioning our future happiness or unhappiness."

~~ GIL FRONSDAL

CONTINUING OUR DISCUSSION OF PAST LIVES, UNDERSTAND AND addressing what presently holds you back starts with looking at the cause. For many the cause stems from a previous life. We will dive into how to access the memories of past lives, and, how this can help you release blocks in your present life, which will help you heal. I attended a group past life regression session where video cameras were present with the purpose of capturing any supernatural presence of orbs. During the session, my team, or my "peeps" appeared in full force. My regression was remarkable and fascinating.

My Past-Life Regression

With two of my guides I found myself in the place you go before birth. At last count I had six guides. They come in to help me integrate higher dimensional aspects, as well as remove blocks, and, they have taught me what I am sharing with you in this book. One guide has been with me this entire lifetime; another guide has been with me for all my incarnations.

In this still white place we were talking like friends discussing what experiences I would have and why I was coming forth. We sat at a table and I was writing in the pages of my Akashic book, where all my lifetimes have been recorded. As I finished writing, the three of us got up and walked over to what seemed like the edge of this dimension, and I looked down to the world below.

I saw my Mom lying on a hospital bed in labor, giving birth to me. Next, I moved into her womb, and so did the same two guides. I felt love from my Mom as I waited for my birth. I also felt love from my guides. In that moment I knew they were showing me I was not alone on this journey.

I would know what to do when the time was right; they would be guiding me along the way.

I did not experience the birth because it was not important. Knowing what experiences lay ahead; that I was prepared and I would not be alone was significant.

Next, we were instructed to visit a life where we died, and, the death impacted this lifetime. I found myself outside and I looked Mayan, or Peruvian. There were people who did not like my strict teachings, so they captured me while I was away from home and hung me. I felt the sorrow as tears fell down my face. I do believe my Mayan or Peruvian life caused my fear of bringing all my spiritual gifts out. What a blessing to be able to finally release it.

Next we were instructed to connect with our Higher-Self. When I did so, all the guides on my team showed up to support me. All six of them were with me and they felt such love for me. They showed me the future and how all is even better than perfect.

At that point my Dad, Grandmother, and Uncle, entered to say, "Hello," and asked if the music could be more uplifting, because they wanted to dance. I told them to pose for the camera, because the workshop facilitator was taking pictures. Next, I thanked them for showing up. Then, I returned to my body, with a deeper, more thorough understanding of this amazing journey.

Another regression found me in Denmark during the Middle Ages. I saw thatch roofed homes in what looked like a bustling, village. There were people walking, going about their daily business. Then I looked down at my feet. On my feet was a pair of very old worn, leather boots that peered out from under an even older, long, somewhat shabby dress. I was a lady on my way home from the market with food for my children. I arrived at my home, opened the door and walked in. It was modestly furnished in rustic, hand-crafted furnishings.

There were three children inside. I did not recognize them at first, but as I got closer and could see their eyes, I knew exactly who they were. There was a boy at a small table witling wood. He had the same eyes as my husband in this life, and, my husband Don is quite handy in this life, in fact he remolded our current home. Cleaning up the modest, Danish home we lived in was a young, teen girl, about age fifteen. I recognized her to be my youngest sister in this life. Finally, there was another even younger child about six years old. I could tell from her eyes, she was my Mom in my current life. It seemed as if my husband died and left us very poor. But we had the love of each other and the family bond between us was strong.

Next, I saw myself going up the stairs at a church in the center of the village. My oldest daughter was getting married. It was a joyful occasion, and the entire village was there to celebrate. Finally, I found myself back in our meager home, this time in bed with my children surrounding me. In that moment, I was about to take my last breath. The sadness I felt made this all too real, and suddenly I was gone. What a beautiful and simple life it was, one of the simplest I have been shown. They wanted me to see the connection I have to my husband Don, my Mom and one of my sisters. It was such an amazing regression experience because I feel so motherly toward them, and have loving, nurturing relationships with all three of them.

Then I found myself climbing stairs, seven marble stairs. As I ascended them, the bright white light coming from beyond grew even more dazzling. When I arrived at the top stair and looked inside, I saw a library. It was beautiful. The bookcases were massive, going skyward so high I could not even see where they ended. Each bookcase held massive leather-bound books, about eighteen inches high by three to four inches thick. I was in the Akashic Hall and it was a magnificent, glorious place to behold.

I sensed the presence of a being there, but I could not see it until I asked them. A beautiful, angelic being quickly appeared. She wore a white robe glistening with hues of aqua, violet and gold. Her hair was long and black. She seemed to possess loving, kind attributes like love, and compassion. At the same time I sensed her wisdom, power and strength. She was one of my guides and her name rhymed with Tinkerbelle. She told me I was here to help bring more people into the light and help them awaken. It was finally time for my work to begin. Life has not been the same since for me.

Guiding Yourself Through Past Lives

My Higher-Self guides me through these experiences, without me doing much but observe. However, I know this is not the case for most. So here is an uncomplicated, fun exercise you can do to help you begin remembering your past lives. You will actually be doing self-hypnosis but, don't worry it is very easy to do. When you are alert yet relaxed and calm, basically in a light, meditative state is the best time to do this.

If this process is different for you than I have described below, and the screen does not go black, see yourself back at the doorway where it all began. Open it walking backward the way you came in, seeing it exactly like it was. As you walk, tell yourself you will arrive completely refreshed, with full recall of the past life experience.

An important point I need to make; remember throughout all your lifetimes you have lived on both sides of the track, you have experienced doing good for others and not so good in some lives. So, if a past life presents itself to you that you find disturbing, do not attach to it or make it more important than necessary.

Your authentic self is love and this was simply lessons being learned. Know you are surrounded in love and you may leave whenever you like. This process should be easy, so if you are having a tough go at it, stop and try again another day. Also, do not participate in these sessions too close together. Give yourself one or more weeks off between sessions; allowing you to review your notes and discover any patterns that may reveal more truths to you. Remember, doing the meditation regression too often can cause you to create inaccurate memories. Here is what to do:

- Start by getting quiet. Sit comfortably with your feet and hands uncrossed, or lay down in a quiet, darkened room.
- Close your eyes and begin focusing on your breath. Breathe in through your mouth and out through your nose.
- Remember, your subconscious cannot tell what is real or made up, so go with it.
- Put a protective white light around you for safety.
- Envision a white, enveloping light all around you. See it in your mind's eye.
- See the light shining on your feet, your legs, your knees, your thighs, your torso and arms, your neck, your face and finally, your head. This white light is protecting you from all negative influences. It is the loving essence of God, providing a warm, sparkling mistiness all around you, cocooning you in its brilliance, protecting you from anything that might possibly be harmful.
- See it in your mind. Feel it's warmth and invite it to wash over you.
- Repeat to yourself with each inhalation, "I am breathing in powerful protective energy. This energy is building an aura of protection around me. This aura protects me at all times in every way."
- Do this with intention five times, quietly or aloud.
- Make sure you concentrate on visualizing, feeling the energy, making it brighter and more powerful with each in-breath and out-breath.

- Take the next color that comes into your mind, and repeat " I am breathing in powerful protective energy" until you are ready to continue.

- Next, imagine yourself in a long hallway with a large, intricate door at the end. See this hallway in as much detail as you can, whatever comes to your mind is fine. Your hallway may be all gold, or white, Gothic like a cathedral, or mystical with crystals, or a forest floor with fairies leading. The choice is yours. Create your hallway the same way in your mind every time you do this exercise.

- Imagine this hallway with the expectation that when you get to the end, reach the big door, turn the knob and enter, you will discover a past life.

- As you begin walking down the hallway, do so with purpose. See your feet touch the ground with each step you take, visualizing every aspect of your journey, from the smells and sounds of your surroundings, to the beautiful colors you may see.

- As you reach the end of the hallway prepare yourself to grasp the doorknob.

- Take hold of the doorknob when you're ready. Feel the texture of the knob, and the sound it makes as you turn it. Breathe now and push the door open.

- As I mentioned your subconscious does not know the difference between what is real or imagined, so accept the initial thing you observe as you open the door as a scene from a past life.

- What you see will be as individual as you are. There is no wrong or right just go with what shows up.

- The first thing you see may be as abstract as a color, or, a driftnet. It could be as vivid as you riding horseback.

- Take whatever you see as the foundation of this past life. Build upon it. Feel it.
- Hold the imagery in your mind and open up to it, accepting whatever arises.
- The vision will begin taking shape as you walk deeper into it. Perhaps you are a soldier in old England riding a horse through the countryside, for example.

Are You Wearing Shoes?

When I experienced my first regression, I doubted it until I felt the loss of a loved one. Then it became very real for me. So, be patient with yourself, taking it one step at a time. Know you are remembering a past life experience, even if it feels like you are making it up.

It can be helpful in the beginning to look down at your feet.
- Are you wearing shoes?
- If so, what do they look like?
- Are they sandals like in Roman days?
- Or, perhaps riding boots?
- Maybe you are not wearing any footwear.

After you focus on your feet then look slightly upward and become aware of what you are wearing; perhaps a leather tunic, a billowy Renaissance dress, or, a wool military uniform. When you remember something and you feel confident it is your truth, you now have something to build upon and pick up from this point the next time.

Begin each of your past life regression sessions with something you have already seen. You will know you have finished because the scene stops. For me it is like the movie is over and the screen suddenly turns black with no credits or anything, just black. Keep a journal, to note each experience so you recognize patterns as they develop.

The more you practice the better you will become. Remember to take breaks between sessions. To truly discover your past, you must believe what you are seeing. Do not let your ego get in the way. Do not allow negative voices to tell you it is not real, or, you are a little crazy. Be ready, dear reader, to find and accept the truth as you see, feel and hear it. As you do, you will have an amazing epiphany, recognizing a past lifetime is influencing your present one.

Addressing Issues as they are Revealed

If you discover you have an issue, if there is a matter of an incompletion remaining from a previous life, or, even from your childhood, now is the time to address it. Your purpose with this exercise is discovering what may be lingering and limiting you from your past lives. Also, it is about how you can mend, heal and continue through your path as issued are revealed. To continue down this path of awakening, you must release what no longer serves you. Or, you may continue unconsciously recreating the same limiting beliefs until you finally let go.

There are so many techniques available to help you complete and heal past life experiences by yourself. Or, you can work with a qualified specialist who understands past life incompletions, has training and can help you. With a little research you can discover what will work best for you, like:

- The Emotion Code
- Body Code Healing System
- Emotional Freedom Technique and more.

The purpose of this book is helping you navigate your journey by providing effective ways to awaken yourself. I share my personal experiences to support and inspire you to trust the process, as I have. This has worked most successfully for me.

By now, you may be wondering how you accumulated so many blockages in the first place. There are about thirteen emotions which you can express at any given moment including: bliss, love, peace, mastery, passion, playful, hope, fear, hopeless, hate, anger, repulsion, grief, and pain. When you have an experience where one of these emotions is felt and you are unable to fully express the emotion you are feeling, then the emotion becomes blocked or what is known as a blockage.

Over time, yes even lifetimes, these blockages can impact you in a negative way. For example, imagine you were hurt as a young boy. You felt the tears welling up and wanted to cry. However your Dad stopped you by saying, "Big boys don't cry! Suck it up." Or, "Don't be a sissy!" You held all the emotions you were feeling inside. Those emotions went unexpressed, thus they were suppressed within you. If that hurt continues to go unexpressed it can create a blockage and be carried into your next life.

The best, most empowering scenario is expressing your emotions as they occur, breathing through the feelings. Unfortunately this is not always the case.

- A good place to begin is always with gratitude. Giving thanks allows you to clear years of repressed feelings because your emotional body is linked to your heart and soul. Gratitude raises the vibration of your emotional body, thus allowing for the release of these feelings.

- Another way to release blocked emotions is by expressing yourself through writing. Journaling is popular for a reason; it allows you to go deep into the recesses of your mind and put words to what you are feeling, why you are feeling it, and, what sensations you are experiencing in your body.

Once you recognize something, it becomes easier to release. As you surrender and let go of old, blocked emotions, and the meaning you have given them, you begin noticing how the energy of your written words begins to free your trapped emotions.

Struck by Lightning

I remember one night lying in bed and I started vibrating. Suddenly a bolt of white light, like a lightning bolt appeared. I watched as it came through the roof of my home, through the ceiling in my bedroom and struck my heart. I felt my heart shift deeply. It lasted a few moments before I drifted off to sleep again. The following morning when I woke up, I noticed my chest actually hurt. Then I remembered what happened in the middle of the night.

Open Your Heart

You must open your heart and love unconditionally to advance down the path of light. At that time I was unfamiliar with emotional blocks. If I had an emotional heart block previously, I am sure in that moment it was removed.

Chapter Seven

Transformation: Becoming
The Butterfly

*"It's not our personality, our lower self
that decides the timing of our awakening
but our higher self."*

~~ TANIS HELLIWELL

ALL MY EXPERIENCES HAVE CLEARLY MOVED ME ON my person-al path of awakening and transformation. It does not matter what experiences you have, as long as you stay in your heart and allow your Higher-Self to be your guide. However your awakening happens, know that it is perfect. As I write this chapter, I contemplate the fact that my home is on the market for sale. Currently, I am not only experiencing a spiritual transformation but a physical one as well.

To my surprise, after living in this house with my husband for eleven happy years, there is a heightened sense of both peace and excitement knowing all is truly well. I already know the perfect new home will appear and this move will happen with ease and grace. So, I emphasize the importance of your willingness to let go of the illusion that events and circumstances are supposed to happen a certain way. Your authentic awakening requires you to embrace the notion there are components to the process based on trust alone. Surrendering is where you will discover and become your authentic, true self. To a great extent, the removing of my heart block or heart wall described in the previous chapter led to my transformation. Follow your heart; it is smarter than you think.

The process of awakening has many steps, lessons and skills to help you through each stage. I use the word "stage" because there are so many. After all, how many lifetimes have you lived? All the layers holding you in this false illusion of separation, lack and limitation must be cleared so the connection to your true self can be made again.

Lucid Dreaming

One such skill is the ability to have lucid dreams. I remember when I began having lucid dreams. Lying on the sofa with my husband watching television, I would fall asleep. While in the dream, dreaming, I was still aware of the movie on television, and aware my husband was moving about. Afterwards I had a clear remembrance of all three things. This experience is commonly referred to as Lucid Dreaming.

So, lucid dreaming is an awareness of the fact you are dreaming. This awareness can range from a slight, faint perception like the experience I described above, to something momentous and greater than any experience you have had in a fully awake state. Lucid dreams usually occur while you are in the middle of a regular dream. Suddenly you realize that you are dreaming. Once you realize this, you have the ability to control your dreams. You can actually rewind it and change the outcome, which is the most essential part of lucid dreaming.

Early one June I was sleeping peacefully, and I woke up to use the bathroom. Afterward, I went back to bed at about five AM in the morning. I kept hearing a word repeated over and over again in my head. The word was "Popuwaw," and it kept repeating like a consistent drumbeat in my head. I never heard the word before and I had no idea what it meant, or, how to spell it. As I drifted off to an altered state of sleep, I found myself on a tropical island. I walked toward what looked like a tiki hut. There was a woman sitting at one of the bar stools, so I took the vacant seat since there were only two seats at this tiki bar. An older, Polynesian-looking gentleman turned around with a white plate of food, and said his name was Popuwaw. He had food for my soul. He picked up an old-looking wooden staff and began walking. I followed him down a long, wooded path. As I did he began pointing to different plants and flowers on both sides of the path with his staff. We walked and as he pointed to all the different plants, I asked if I was supposed to remember the names of these plants and their uses. He did not answer. We came to a clearing, and a stage appeared. Once again, it was like a long tiki hut with about a hundred people there. Seven elders stood on the stage. They were in charge. The elders began reading from a book;

my guess is it was the Akashic records. As they read, they recounted the lives of the one-hundred people gathered. When they came to my name it seemed like what was prevalent in other records was read not in mine. After a moment they paused and looked at me. They said I was the one. As they spoke, everyone became more youthful in appearance. They all bowed toward me, including Popuwaw who became youthful in his look as well. Suddenly there was an overwhelming sense of love and belonging. I felt a powerful connection to the point of wanting to stay. But the time had come for me to leave and Popuwaw escorted me back on the path. As he did so, he told me, "You can return at any time, for you know the way." Moments later I found myself back in bed with tears rolling down my face. I could not go back to sleep, my curiosity got the best of me.

I wanted to know what this experience meant. I certainly wanted to know the meaning of his name. It turns out Popuwaw is the Pawpaw tree: a Polynesian tree which grows in some parts of North America. The tree contains amazing medicinal properties. My conclusion is the energy in the Spirit of this living plant wanted me to know about these properties for a future use, perhaps to slow or reverse conditions brought on with age.

Though in an altered state of sleep, I was clearly aware what took place in my dream state to the point of remembering and questioning the messages I received.

Lucid dreaming offers a virtual storehouse of messages, catapulting you through the awakening process. Here are suggestions to help you develop your own lucid dreaming:

- First, figure out the best time for you to have a lucid dream. Your awareness of your personal sleep schedule will allow you to arrange your sleep pattern to induce lucid dreams. For me, the ideal time is between four and five AM, in the morning. Are you surprised?

- Lucid dreams are strongly associated with REM, or rapid eye movement sleep. REM sleep is more abundant just before our final awakening. This means they most commonly occur right before you wake up. We usually remember the dreams we interrupt, so it may be a good idea to force yourself to wake up.

- Technique One: Set your alarm clock to wake you four and one half, six, or seven and one half hours after falling asleep. When you are awakened by the alarm clock, try remembering as much of your dream as possible. When you think you have remembered as much as you can, return to sleep. Imagine you are in your previous dream, and becoming aware you are dreaming. Say to yourself, "I'm aware I'm dreaming," or something similar. Repeat this until you feel you got it. Then drift off to sleep. If random thoughts pop up as you try falling back asleep, repeat the imagining, self-suggestion part, and try again. Do not worry if you think it is taking a long time. The longer it takes, the more likely it will "sink in," and the more likely you will experience a lucid dream.

- Technique Two: Once again set your alarm clock to five hours after you typically fall asleep. Go to sleep. After waking up, stay up for an hour with your mind focused on lucidity and only lucidity. Now allow yourself to drift back to sleep.

There are a few aids to facilitate your lucid dreaming process:

- Start a dream journal: I keep one journal for everything, dreams visions, meditations, everything. When something occurs outside my "normal awake state", I write it down or record it. This helps you spot abnormalities. It also aids in dream recollection.

- Teleporting is fun: Close your eyes, spin your dream body and envision a brand new landscape. Then open your eyes. This skill is invaluable to practice and acquire. Before you know it, you will develop the capability to do anything in your dreams. You are only limited by your beliefs.

- Try Vitamin B6: It can increase the vividness of your dreams.

As I developed my ability to dream lucidly, I continued my personal transformation. The vibrating, pulsing and colors swirling in my vision grew stronger.

What is Transformation?

What does transformation really mean? According to Webster's Dictionary transformation is the act or an instance of transforming. Or, it can be described as the state of being transformed.

Spiritually speaking, transformation is a term defined broadly as profound changes in the way people understand, approach, and experience whatever they hold as sacred. The term spiritual transformation is used to identify what is understood widely in the psychology of religious literature as a "conversion experience." The mystical experience is perhaps best thought of as a specific type of spiritual transformation.

As I found myself experiencing my own spiritual transformation, at times it felt I was losing control of my life and my mind. I even found myself questioning my identity. Now I know these feelings were my personality's fear of losing control. Actually, enduring through this experience is a true indication of strength, spiritual growth and emotional maturity. All these are a natural part of the transformational process.

Many cultures and world religions speak of this doubt and a sense of losing control:

- In the Old Testament of the Bible it is referred to as, "the dark night of the soul."
- The 23rd Psalm of the Bible speaks of this journey as, "going through the valley of the shadow of death."
- In ancient Greece, Egypt, India and other cultures, schools of wisdom helped individuals through this process. Individuals were taken into seclusion and taught, "…the Inner Mysteries, which are the spiritual truths on which our world is founded."

Must I Transform Spiritually?

You may ask, "Is it necessary to undergo a spiritual transformation?" Yes, it is because the purpose of our transformation is to become a conscious Creator on the planet in accordance with Divine Will. The wonderful thing about the process is we are designed to succeed. So wherever you are, is perfect. Each of us is given exactly what is needed to assist us in our transformation. I received a great deal of assistance from my guides. From seeing amazing colors every time I closed my eyes, making spirals and different shapes, to seeing images and pictures.

In Chapter Two I shared an experience which started with images that appeared flipping forward every twenty to thirty seconds like a child's ViewMaster toy. You may recall the visions shifted to an experience of "bleeding" to remove the sins of my fathers and finally a Gatekeeper gave me the key to an astonishing blue-violet vortex in the cosmos with a million stars glittering all around. As I shared in that chapter, I was being tuned up, prepared for what they would teach me.

That experience, my affirming prayers and meditation afterwards with my entire team of Spirit guides gave me a tremendous sense of confidence, empowerment and purpose. However, I still had an important question, *"Where am I from?"* What returned back to me was the old Biblical adage, *"Seek and ye shall find."*

As I was waking up one morning I was greeted by an eye looking at me and it was not my husband. So, I closed my eyes to shrug it off. When I opened them again this time two eyes were looking at me now. Then a face appeared, and then a body. It was not human, but I recognized her anyway.

From Spirit Energy to Form

It was my God-Mother or my very first mother as we go from being Spirit-energy to form. She lay there and I moved into her arms. I felt her warm embrace, her fingers long and extremely soft, as they cradled me. Her love for me was intensely powerful. She knew everything about me, even the fact I did not have children in this life. She is deep purple in color with very long hair. They are known as the long-haired beings.

I knew from this point on, she was with me to assist in my return to higher vibrational consciousness. She is a twelfth dimensional being, and was showing me her love and letting me know I too was becoming my higher dimensional self again.

Everyone will have their own experiences as they awaken and increase their consciousness and vibrational level. I am sharing my experiences with you, not for you to make comparisons, but so you will begin to recognize when you are having your own spiritual experiences or visitations. Transformation does not belong to me alone, but it is for each and every one of us when we are open to it.

As I started teaching classes and doing activations with clients, things started happening to the people I assisted and facilitated. The following story is from one of those clients. She now is a good friend and here is her story of transformation.

A Client's Unvarnished Experience

"I took the red pill," she told me smiling. "I probably could have taken the blue pill, rolled over and went back to sleep. My quest for truth is deeply ingrained. That is the path that I am on. I believe it's inevitable we will all wake up soon.

Seeking like-minded people has been a blessing and led me to wonderful new friends. If it wasn't for them, I'm not sure I could handle this and I'm pretty sure I would have thought I was going crazy instead of awakening.

The first major "ascension symptom" I experienced was the day my leg "disappeared". I could see it but I couldn't feel it. I thought I might be having a stroke. It lasted less than thirty seconds.

I had a Reiki healing and discovered from my Reiki Master, the same thing happened to three other people. Shortly after, I added a new supplement to my routine; blue skate liver oil. It's more powerful for decalcifying the pineal than MSM.

The next morning I got in the shower and closed my eyes under the water. I saw the brightest, glowing green orb. I see colors quite often, especially violet, but this was the brightest, most beautiful to date.

Later I was sitting grounded at my computer and I felt both the male and female chakras outside my head. It was powerful as they came online. That night I connected to Mother Earth and visualized the plants growing and blooming where I usually take my morning walk with my dog, Spirit, and a good friend. The next morning I went for a walk there and yes, overnight the area had bloomed like crazy.

The next morning I got up and grounded myself at my computer. This day I felt a tingling all over my head. Then I went for my usual morning walk. That's when the strangest thing to date happened to me. My whole left arm "disappeared." I could see it and I could move it but I couldn't feel it. My first instinct was to ground myself so I got on my hands and knees.

My friend and walking buddy Lois suggested touching the plants. I ran my left hand across the blooms of a shrub. Each blossom sent a surge of powerful energy all the way up my arm. It almost felt like an electric current running through. When I touched five blossoms, five separate lines of current ran up my arm.

I have never felt anything so strange and wonderful at the same time. I'm an electrician so I know what electric current feels like. It was almost the same, except it didn't hurt.

If it wasn't for the guidance of Reverend Edwige and other friends, I would have come undone. I looked up 'ascension symptoms' when I got home and found out people who reported similar symptoms. Curious thing, all experienced the sensation with the left arm like me. Yesterday was the lunar eclipse with the sun in Taurus and the moon in Scorpio. My sun is in Scorpio and it was almost conjuncted. The moon actually did conjunct my sun the next day. Makes me wonder what will happen next."

If you are to become Conscious Creators and awaken to your full potential, you need to do it on many levels. To transform yourself, transform your work, and, transform your world. To achieve this goal you must first transform yourself so that your fears, judgments, attachments and self-interest do not sabotage your effectiveness.

Chapter Eight:

Spiritual Gifts

"I say to you, he who believes in me will also do the works I do: and greater works than these he will do."

~~ JESUS (JOHN 14)

SPIRITUAL GIFTS ARE FASCINATING AND MYSTERIOUS AT THE same time. More and more abilities were awakening within me as my vibration continued increasing. I came to learn it was all part of my awakening process. In this chapter, we will dive into spiritual gifts, special abilities and how you can to develop them with ease.

What was Lost, Now is Found

I believe these gifts are part of what you and I accomplished and completed in past lives. We are in the process of remembering the gifts we lost along the way, for nothing is truly new. As a result, I believe the idea of gifts is better when termed, "abilities." Since you were given these abilities eons ago, all you have to do now is remember.

In Corinthians 12:7-11, a spiritual gift is defined as something given to each of us so we can help each other. The Spirit gives:

- To one person the ability to help with wise advice
- To another Spirit gives a message of special knowledge
- The same Spirit gives great faith to another
- To someone else Spirit gives the gift of healing.
- One person is given the power to perform miracles
- Another person receives the ability to prophesy.
- Someone else receives the ability to discern whether a message is from the Spirit of God or from another Spirit
- One person receives the ability to speak in unknown languages; another is given the ability to interpret what is said.

Only the one Great Spirit or God Energy distributes all these gifts. God alone decides which gift each person gains. Remember, you were given some of these gifts lifetimes ago. Though it all may seem new or quite foreign, it is yours to master once again.

Hear these words and awaken to all you possess; all your authentic self holds inside. Growing up in the Catholic Church I was not raised with the concept of spiritual gifts, but as I grew more in alignment with my Higher-Self my spiritual abilities started waking up on their own. The healing flame ignited in my palms one day while meditating. At the time, I didn't know what was happening. The Universe in its infinite wisdom always sends the right person or being at the perfect time to help.

This instance was no exception. Confirmation came from someone I deeply regarded as a spiritual teacher. Before I knew it my Higher-Self was guiding me to stand in my power, so I did. I put my hands above the top of each person's head, more precisely, atop the crown. This is the chakra at the top of the head. At times I am guided to place my hands there and I see a portal or vortex open above the head. I feel and see energy come in. From that place, energy moves through your body going where it's needed.

One time when I was doing this energy work, my Spirit connected with the Spirit of the person I was working on and we flew out into the cosmos together. It was simply amazing, and completely unexpected. When we returned, we looked at each other and simply laughed out loud exclaiming unity consciousness feels like this for us.

What seems so remarkable is when I do this work; I never know exactly what will happen. It could be a physical healing, removing blocks, activating higher chakras, and seeing amazing colors. I can even feel when a heart wall is shattered, or, if someone is ready for an activation to move them forward in their awakening process.

Take a Glimpse at Your Higher-Self

I remember being on a conference call with twenty people. I was not the facilitator or leader of the call. Rather I was simply there to hold the space of love. Lo and behold, I got a glimpse of my Higher-Self: a pure white being around twenty feet high. Suddenly I began pulsating, breaking out in a sweat, rocking back and forth and feeling pain all at the same time. Something was happening, but I was confused what it was.

When the facilitator of the conference call became aware what was happening, she instructed everyone to pause, shifting their awareness to me, while sending love and appreciation to me. In that moment I felt a shift in my left leg. All the pain was gone. My Higher-Self released the negative energy which was holding the group back. The next day I received a call from one of the women on the call. She told me right before the call she was hunched over in pain. As soon as my experience began, energy which felt like a siphon sucked the pain out from her body completely. I am filled with gratitude and awe every time I witness Spirit working through me.

Imagine if you took the time to genuinely look at your Higher Self. Often we do not even want to look because what we would see is so amazing, so fabulous, so dazzling it almost defies any description with mere words. What would you see? Would you respond with powerful emotions and feelings as I did?

This feels like the perfect place to share a quotation by Marianne Williamson from her book, "A Return to Love." She writes:

"...Our deepest fear is not that we are inadequate.

Our deepest fear is that we are powerful beyond measure.

It is our light, not our darkness, that most frightens us.

We ask ourselves, who am I to be brilliant, gorgeous, talented, fabulous?

Actually, who are you *not* to be?

You are a child of God. Your playing small doesn't serve the world.

There's nothing enlightened about shrinking so that other people won't feel insecure around you.

We are all meant to shine, as children do.

We were born to make manifest the glory of God that is within us.

It's not just in some of us; it's in everyone.

And as we let our own light shine, we unconsciously give other people permission to do the same.

As we're liberated from our own fear, our presence automatically liberates others..."

When you begin accepting and embracing your power and magnificence, letting your light shine in the ways your soul is meant to, you will being vibrating at a higher level.

One gift I did not necessarily care for was dealing with the departed. I discovered I could send the souls of people who had passed on but who had not yet departed into the light, into the light. The first experience was one morning when I was touched gently on my left hand, enough to wake me up. As I awoke, all the colors began moving into my vision. As they did a vortex took shape. I watched the vortex expand into a magnificent blue sky. It was a gorgeous, azure blue with billowy white clouds.

I knew this was how I was to send the Spirit standing next to me into the heavenly realms beyond. I instinctively knew to energetically move it toward the vortex. So I gently guided it with my hands. It moved upward as if on a puff of air. As it did, the vortex gradually disappeared behind it. The love from the light stayed with me throughout the entire day. It was the most joyful love and light one could experience.

Receiving Your Spiritual Gifts

We all have gifts we have received and not known how to best use. When we think about receiving gifts, we know we would like to receive something heartfelt. We also want something we can use, otherwise what is the point? There is such a gift you have already received; it is a gift from God.

How do you become aware of your spiritual gifts?

I believe the first step, is to recognize and acknowledge the gifts of which you already are aware. This is basic and uncomplicated. You cannot develop something you do not know exists. You cannot develop a piece of property if you do not know what it is worth.

My husband and I used to buy "fixer upper" homes, and either sell or rent them. The point is we had to first recognize their potential before cultivating them.

Clients often ask me, "Is it possible to choose my own Spiritual gifts?"

The simple answer is, "No." Your spiritual gift or gifts are based on your soul purpose and what you came forth to do. The more you come in harmony with your purpose, the more your abilities are clearly revealed to you. You do not have to earn your gift, it is yours to unwrap and develop. New abilities or gifts will continue appearing as you grow spiritually and your consciousness expands.

From here, you begin opening up to your Higher-Self who already knows everything. Your personal, spiritual gift will remain unused, idle, and abandoned unless you recognize and use it. How do you recognize it? There are three signs you can use to determine and identify your gifts or abilities:

- The first sign you possess a spiritual gift, is you have an ability to do something your friends, family members or associates do not possess. It could be as simple as having a better voice for singing. This was true for me when I began singing in the school choir at age nine. Perhaps you have the ability to articulate and orate clearly to influence large groups of people.

- The second sign to discover your special, spiritual gift is exercising ability with ease or great facility. You do not force yourself; instead it flows effortlessly from your body or mind. Singing gracefully comes naturally, for example. Giving clear explanations to people is natural for you. Perhaps organizing and maintaining meticulous accounting records is effortless. Or maybe you have another gift that comes easily like working with animals or helping people resolve conflicts amicably.

- The third sign you have a gift is you exercise this gift with no thought of gain. The principle observed is you have been given this gift freely, and freely you give it to others. If you sing extraordinary well and you join singing contests to win money, your gift becomes a talent. In a similar way, if you explain clearly to people and use this gift to earn a degree in teaching, then your gift becomes a talent.

Using your talents to make money is perfectly fine. There can and should be a reciprocal exchange of value. However, receiving nothing other than gratitude should be your motive. If you exercise your gift only for the sake of earning something, it becomes a mere talent. You do well to seek ye first, and allow all else to be added unto you.

The Act of Gratitude and Thanks

Once you recognize your gift, give thanks to Spirit for it. The act of gratitude is not something you do just once and you are done. Every day, remember to express gratitude for this gift, or gifts. Every moment of the day be observant about remaining in this attitude of gratitude. People often ask me, "How often do you pray?" Without fail, I reply, "There is never a time I am not in the awareness of Spirit, or, in gratitude for the abundance of good surrounding me."

Many people feel the gift is their right. As a result they unfortunately take it for

granted. Such feelings lead to not fully appreciating the importance of the gift, or,

acknowledging God, the giver of all gifts. In these instances, the appreciation and

acknowledgment is only an occasional thought. A genuinely grateful heart is

connected as one with an abiding sense of thankfulness to the giver of all. Before and

after using your abilities, give thanks to the Great Spirit, or God. Spiritual gifts are not

always as obvious as you may think, like:

- The power to heal or speak in tongues.
- The gift of design and making spaces beautiful
- Some gifts are subtle, like the gift of asking; or of listening.
- Perhaps you have the gift of hearing, using a still, small voice
- The gift of holding the space of love.
- The gift of avoiding vain repetition.
- The gift of not passing judgment.

We are all here to serve in our own unique way. Once you have recognized your

spiritual gift or ability, it is time to develop it. People with musical gifts tend to practice playing instruments or composing music more rather than less than people without

those gifts. Consider athletes; people gifted at a sport like basketball or soccer. They

play basketball more, and practice more drill skills than people with little ability, They

simply love the game, so even though they have a gift they get even better. It is one of

the happy burdens of owning a gift.

How do you develop your gift? That is easy: practice, practice and more practice. This also applies to the gift of healing. When I was finally guided to stand in my power, and first began laying hands on people to heal, I had to practice what I know. The other important practice in developing your spiritual gifts is to become more holy. This means raising your vibration, your frequency and becoming more loving. Become the Christed being you are and watch what happens.

Energy, Vibration and Frequency

This path leads me to share a more focused look at energy, vibration, and frequency. Everything in the Universe is energy, and all energy exists at different levels of vibration and frequency. We are moving from third dimensional consciousness to fourth dimension and higher, as is the earth. Consciousness and vibrational frequency are perfectly correlated. When you are operating at a lower frequency, you are lower in consciousness. Your perception is dulled, and you view the world through a foggy lens.

When you operate at a higher frequency, you are higher in consciousness, your perception is heightened and you see things more clearly as you ascend higher and higher. Just as when you soar skyward in an airplane, the higher you climb, the larger your picture. As you break through the clouds the brighter your horizon becomes.

Raising your vibration allows you to connect more directly with your Higher-Self. Because your Higher-Self vibrates at a higher level, too. Creating and using this relationship to your Higher-Self allows for information to be more easily accepted by your consciousness, and then fully actualized. In other words, once you begin raising your vibration, you can better understand life and everything in general. You will feel more at peace, in touch, connected, and happier.

What exactly is energy? Everything in our Universe is made up of energy and matter. You have already read many times so far in this book about vibration, or, things having a vibrational level. So you have probably already gleaned the idea the level at which you vibration is critically important, even if you are still unsure what it is and how it works.

Everything energy and matter has an energetic vibration. It may be a high vibrational level or a low one. Energetic vibrations attract similar vibrations. If you have heard of the Law of Attraction you understand the principle of like attracts like. More accurately stated it is closer to like energy attracts more like energy. The human body and our outer experience as we look around us is comprised of 99 percent energy and one percent matter.

What I find remarkable is most people have a tendency to focus 99 percent of their attention and their consciousness on what we visually see, matter. This is shockingly less than one percent of what we are working with and what is out there for you, every day. The invisible energy, the 99 percent, and its energetic vibration, actually has the greatest weight and pull on your life, your results, and your outcomes. Your reality or outpicturing in your life is a direct reflection of what your energetic vibration is attracting.

There are two forms of energy in the Universe: kinetic energy and potential energy. Kinetic energy is energy in motion. Potential energy is stored or motionless energy. Kinetic energy is working for you right now. Potential energy is stored away in matter waiting for direction from someone or something.

You have as much energy as you need to perform the goals you think about and dream about. In fact, you have unlimited power and energy. However, this energy will not be revealed until you raise your level of vibration to the level of consciousness in which this energy exists.

What you see in your human experience is matter; solid, liquid, or gaseous. Solid matter consists of tightly packed molecules with a low vibrational level in a specific shape and size. Solid matter is dense, heavy, and restricted. Remember in an earlier chapter we discussed how your choice of words impacts you? The molecules found in liquid matter are more spread out and fluid thus they operate at a higher vibrational level. Molecules in gaseous substances, like steam or the air we breathe, are the most spread out. They are free to flow in all directions giving them the highest vibration of all three.

The higher your energetic vibrational level, the lighter, happier, and freer you feel and gradually become. Your thoughts, intentions, and emotions are a strong indicator of your vibrational level. This is also influenced by your experiences and environments.

When you become conscious of your vibration and its role in your life, you can choose to raise your vibrational level by choosing positive thoughts and emotions which feel good to you and are in alignment with the greater good of all. Regardless of your conscious thoughts, destiny plays an central part. You may recall where I wrote in the pages of my Akashic record and I was shown all I was to do and accomplish in this life. Your level of consciousness and vibrational level become significant in how your destiny plays out, and whether or not it is miserable or miraculous.

For example, jumping back to the car accident with my Mom I shared in Chapter two: It was my destiny to awaken at that time in my life. Since my vibrational level was not as high then as it is now, I became a vibrational match to the car accident. It evolved into my personal "chaos-into-harmony" moment. It could have played different ways, because the only fact in my Akashic record was for me to awaken. The "how" I was to awaken, or, when I was supposed to awaken was totally up to me. Or, perhaps I should say when "my vibration" was supposed to awaken.

Lower vibrations usually result in more suffering and often include negative:

- Thoughts and actions like complaining, excuses and blaming
- Emotions like anger, fear, shame, jealously, guilt and sadness
- Outcomes like conflict, pain, illness, loss, accident, trauma and drama

Higher vibrations result in more love and joy including positive:

- Thoughts like gratitude, appreciation, and abundance
- Emotions like peace, joy, compassion and acceptance and
- Outcomes like health, happiness, success and prosperity

Most important is *how you feel*, vibrationally speaking. This makes a big difference. The emotional vibration you emit all the time attracts situations and scenarios to match the feeling you put out into the world. We have all heard the phrase, *"What you put out is what you get back."* The Universe is completely neutral; it does not favor anyone.

The Universe simply gives you precisely what you ask for, vibrationally speaking. The Universe, God, only vibrates in one way and in one direction. That direction is toward love and flow. You are either in the flow or not. God does not pick and choose for you. By what you vibrate to, you pick and choose.

The higher your vibrational frequency, the more you are able to comprehend because you are allowing a greater flow of Life Force coursing through your mind and body. Vibrational frequency depends greatly on the amount of Life Force you are allowing to channel through. Life Force can similarly be characterized as God Energy, Intelligence, or love. It is continually emanating from Source.

The lower your vibrational frequency, the less you are able to comprehend because your ego is restricting the flow of life force/God energy and intelligence/love through your mind and body. Your fearful ego instead uses judgment and resistance to choke off the flow. To overcome this, you must override your ego. You must override your resistance and make a powerful commitment to allow love to flow through you no matter what else is happening around you. This commitment to vibration and allowing love to flow through is essential.

The more you allow the essence of God to flow through your mind and body, the higher your vibrational frequency becomes, and, the more creative you will become giving way to a more joyful, more authentic, more loving and empowered you. The lower you are in vibrational frequency, the fewer creative ideas and empowerment you will experience and utilize. Why? Because your ego is choking off the flow, less of God's essence is allowed to flow through your mind and body.

Allow your vibrational energy to move into the flow of love, receiving, joy and peace. Higher vibrational frequency not only makes you wiser and more powerful, it moves you out of struggle, turmoil and pain. It places you in the realm of joy, ease, peace, and harmony. The key to claiming wisdom, creativity, empowerment and every possible blessing is all held within the conscious steps of raising your vibrational frequency. This is assured by allowing more love to flow.

There are many ways to raise your vibration to a place of love, compassion, appreciation, and abundance. Below is a list of the more obvious. What brings you the most joy? What makes your heart sing? Do it now. Here is a partial list to motivate and inspire you to raise your vibrational level.

21 Powerful Ways to Increase Your Vibrational Level

- Meditate, be still and know that I AM. Connect with your Higher-Self.
- Focus on raising your vibration. It requires practice, practice, practice.
- Think happy thoughts all the time. The choice is yours.
- Become present and mindful, living in the now. Stop living on autopilot.
- Set positive intentions daily. Choose to live by intention, not by default
- Bring your awareness to your energy body, your aura
- Connect with your inner body. What does your inner voice tell you?
- Bond with nature: sunshine, water, dirt, fire, plants and animals. See God in all.
- Listen to and create expressive music. Those who sing pray twice.
- Dance, play, move, exercise, stretch, jump and raise your endorphin levels.
- Read, write, journal, learn, explore, and travel. Let your creative juices flow.
- Inspire yourself and inspire others. Be the best you can in this moment.

- Seek higher levels of consciousness and truth. The truth will set you free.
- Smile, stand up tall, and acknowledge others with your eyes. You are the temple.
- Appreciate everything around you now, after all you created it.
- Share your compassion and love with others. Be it first and then receive it.
- Forgive and release easily and often. Heal thyself first.
- Try new things; challenge yourself; step outside your comfort zone and expand.
- Eat right, drink pure water, avoid fluoride and chlorine. Be a good steward.
- Do kind acts of service to others. Give without expectation, it is a blessing.
- Acknowledge your success, and the success of others, attracting more to you.

The operating principle here is he or she who has something and can be trusted with embracing and taking good care that thing will get to have more and more of it. As you embrace and cultivate your abilities you will begin feeling more confident and empowered. When that happens, you draw to you more success and more opportunities to live a life here in this experience that upwardly spirals from one successful, joyful, peaceful, silly, prosperous, abundant moment to another. From this point forward there is no turning back. Your light will shine too brightly to dim. Before you know it your soul purpose will begin revealing itself to you.

Chapter Nine:

Soul Purpose: Why Am I Here Again?

Your Soul is always there. Its home is at the heart of the Universe. Every good thing you have ever done is from your Soul. But if you sense that you've been seeking your real reason for being on the earth at this time, there's no better way to know why you are here than having your Soul share your Purpose with you. When you know your purpose, your life transforms from the limitations of your personality to the unlimited energies of your Higher Love."

~~ MASTER CHUNYI LIN

BECAUSE EACH OF US IS ENCODED FOR SUCCESS, discovering your soul purpose is a fascinating feature of your journey to conscious awakening. Our purpose, like our unique fingerprints is written on your soul. Be willing to step out on faith and move forward with resolve and dedication.

If clarity is your heartfelt intention, it will come a little closer with each step you take. Your Higher-Self is standing by to assist you, but you must meet at the half-way point. Every day I ask my Higher-Self to be the "Divine Director" of my material experience, and I mean it sincerely every time I make the request. There are moments when I am unsure if I am being shown something of importance. However, my guides and Higher-Self always come through providing more signs, so eventually I understand. Stay open and expect the unexpected and the wondrous, all the time. Allow life to be your guide, paying attention to the signs and markings around you. Each step you take brings you closer to remembering and discovering your essence, which is who you are.

Fearlessness is the Key

The message here is about fearlessness. Release your fears and anxieties about how things should look and feel in your world. I had to let go of my expectations and become fearless. In fact the more I let go of old programs, old beliefs, the more I could connect with Spirit, and hence, the more I was shown.

I felt a definite touch on my right side, like being shaken to wake up early one morning. I replied, "Yes," and before I knew it, I was standing in a place full of stunning white-gold light and vital energy. Before my eyes appeared a long table, twelve feet or more in length. It had a luster to it like marble, or crystal.

I watched as light beings appeared. They looked like elders and I was unable to see their faces clearly. But I sensed abundant wisdom and love within each one. I also noticed their facial features were not necessarily human-looking. They were dressed in white, sitting around the table, one at each end. The others sat along the back of the table so they all were facing me. I looked down at myself, and noticed I was dressed in white, too. They reflected on my actions and gave support and approval. Yes, I was finding my way. Indeed, I was becoming enlightened.

I came to learn they were the council of twelve. These twelve beings created the basic building blocks which allowed worlds to unfold. They maintain the system's integrity, making certain the fabric is not ripped, torn or shred. They came to see things run smoothly within the boundaries of their creation. The consciousness of the Universe split within these beings hold vital resonance for the Universe.

Watch Support Flood In

Live with your soul purpose and the world will support you on all levels. Yes, all who are in the non-physical world will finally see you. If you seek spiritual enlightenment, you first must seek to discover your soul purpose in life. Your soul purpose is the reason you were placed on earth this lifetime. Or, it can be more easily understood by saying your soul purpose is what you should strive to accomplish. Once you know your soul purpose, you can seek spiritual enlightenment discovering the best path to reach your goal. Briefly, your soul purpose is the finish line, your legacy or, what you hope to leave behind when you make your transition and leave this lifetime.

Complementing your soul purpose, your spiritual enlightenment can be the map or direction you should comprehend to finish. When you say you have no idea what your soul purpose is, that is untrue. We all have an idea. In many cases it is much closer to our current reality than we realize. You often cannot consciously see it. Many times along the path of enlightenment you make choices and decisions you think are good ones, only discover a particular choice was not in alignment with your true life purpose. This is not necessarily bad. After all, every experience has a lesson. Honestly, you need to detach from the false notion of right, wrong, black, white, good or bad. That is the old paradigm. It is time for you to move into oneness. Those maligned beliefs and decisions can leave an energetic stamp, resulting in emotional or spiritual blockages. This is why it is so important to remove them.

Goals vs. Purpose

Buckminster Fuller was a twentieth century systems theorist, futurist and author. He said the reason we set goals is to keep us active and in motion. However our goals are not always in alignment with our purpose. Our purpose is generally 90 degrees off from the goals we consciously set for ourselves. The example Fuller gives is the bumble bee. It flies forward collecting nectar, but the true purpose of the bee is cross-pollenization which is off 90 degrees as it collects pollen on its legs, moving from flower to flower.

A modern example is the jet airplane. Experts say jets are off-course 95 percent of the time, constantly making minor course corrections to eventually reach their destination. You are the same as the bee or the jet plane. You may not be aware your true soul purpose is off 90 degrees from the goal you are working on now. Similar to the jet airplane, it may take many small course corrections along the way to arrive at your destination, or in this case, the fulfillment of your soul purpose.

One day while pulling up to the water wellness store I used to own, I got a flat tire. I was parked safely, so this was a minor event. For some reason I let it bother me, taking me out of my heart space and into a mindset of agitation, aggravation, and annoyance. The flat tire was changed, so I made it on time to my next appointment that day. The store was busy and all was well.

At the wee, magical hour of 4:13 AM in the early morning stillness, I was awakened by a voice outside me saying, *"Disconnect from an uneven temper."*

I jumped up, startled, since my husband was out of town and I was home alone. I replied, "Hello, can you repeat that?"

The voice repeated, *"Disconnect from an uneven temper."*

I said, "Oh you're talking about the event yesterday with my flat tire?" I allowed it to move me from my heart space and give my annoyed ego power.

It said, *"Love is all there is."*

Stay in the Heart Space of Love

Going forward, I always observe without attaching. I stay in the space of my heart knowing love is real. Anything which causes you or me to remain outside that space is an illusion. So, how does our past help us understand our true self? Our soul's future? More importantly, how can we transform our desire into something satisfying if we are unclear how our desire might manifest? There is no singular answer but I will share what my experiences have taught me and my clients.

Our soul's purpose or destiny does not happen spontaneously. It is mostly a series of vignettes, or stories, that stand out as pivotal moments in your life. Looking back you see clearly each experience like a brick support-ing the foundation of your life. When the bricks are sufficiently placed, you begin seeing the outline of "your house." Even though you know building the house is work, this inspires you to continue. You get to decide if the work is easy or hard. You can choose to remain enthusiastic; after all, the light at the end of the tunnel is flickering for you. Best of all, you can make changes as you go, knowing the house's foundation will not be shaken by any adjustments necessary along the way to make it a place of joy in which to live.

The same holds true for your spiritual path connecting you to your Higher-Self. Throughout the chapters of this book, I have shared the foundational work I did to become enlightened. I believe if you take positive steps it will transform you, too.

Drawing Closer to Enlightenment

It is about meditating, visualizing and continuing to heal past hurts and patterns which no longer serve you. Use your life lessons as those pivotal moments, those vignettes, to propel you forward. Embrace your daily spiritual practices, opening and living a heart-centered life to understand the power of your words, bringing you closer to your conscious awakening and enlightenment. Become mindful and stop living on autopilot. All this leads to the raising of your conscious awareness. As this happens, more of your true, authentic self will reveal itself to you. The old programs you once held as your truth will melt away.

You will begin recognizing yourself as the eternal immortal being you are. Have faith the Creator of the Universe is ever present; ever watchful; ever faithful; and ever loving, rooting for your success as you increase your vibrations of love, acceptance, joy and peace. Even if you are not always fully present or aware of the creator, God, you were designed to be exactly who you are, from the color of your skin to your knack for crossword puzzles, to running a marathon. It stands to reason your unique DNA combination was designed to serve you on the most important mission of your life; to achieve your soul's purpose.

Spiritual enlightenment is not simply a guideline of what direction to go. It is a guide regarding how to live your life, far more about being then doing. As I discovered, it is about being and living in the space of love. As you become love, you become yourself. As I was becoming my true authentic self, my Higher-Self was becoming a tangible presence within me, even showing up in pictures. To say I felt like I was going a little crazy at times is an understatement. Somehow I remained willing and open to the process as it unfolded. Each night when I went to bed I had no idea what would happen, or, who would show up before waking the next day.

The following experience is what I believe the essence of this journey is about. Even as I share my story with you, I am humbled by it. Know that the flicker of light at the end of the tunnel shines brightly for everyone, including you.

The Pivotal Experience

Weeks before the focal experience leading up to the acceptance of my enlightenment was to happen, I began pulsating and vibrating, yet again, in the early hours one morning. Yes, I woke up. This was becoming my normal practice. The vibrant colors of magenta, blues and greens began moving about in my inner vision. Before I knew it there were orbs entering my inner vision one at a time. They were big and brilliantly, bright white with an overlaid sheen of color on each one. First, a yellow orb came in. I watched as it appeared to move in to me: next a blue orb, a pink orb, and finally, a green orb.

My heart and head began pulsating powerfully. I knew my conscious-ness was returning to my heart. Then on a lunar eclipse a few weeks after the experience with the orbs, while in bed sleeping again, I began pulsating and vibrating once again with intensity. With my inner-vision, I saw en-ergy in the shape of light beings coming in around me, every hour on the hour. Throughout the entire night the beings made contact. I felt a tingling and moving sensation as they worked, like mighty surges of energy, similar to if I was plugged into an electrical socket. It always eased up as they left, continuing the sensations. I continued seeing colors until the next hour when they showed up again. The surging started again. This continued the entire night until I got out of bed in the morning.

Finally, what I felt everything was leading up to, actually came to an energetic peak. I went to bed, and had a difficult time sleeping. There was so much energy surging around me, so I laid awake on my bed in anticipa-tion. Like every other time, I began pulsating, vibrating and seeing colors. This continued for hours. As I focused on the colors and felt the energy, I saw a still point of bright white light descending upon me. As it grew closer it transformed into the shape of a human body. It did not have a face or features, but was a pure white body of light. I watched as it continued descending moving closer and closer until it moved into me.

I was not surprised when I began pulsating and vibrating more intense-ly than ever. I felt a connection between my heart, head and body. This continued several more hours. As much as I wanted to sleep, all I could do was lay there and allow myself to be one with it. I was finally merging with my "I AM "presence, and it was magnificent. That certainly was not my last spiritual, other-worldly experience. Many more experiences have followed since.

I used to question my abilities and soul purpose, asking, "Am I doing enough?" I still was releasing aspects of the ego that seemed to want to hang on; making me feel I was not good enough. Even after all the amazing experiences I had up until then, doubt still crept in. My team had more work to do bringing me to a place of acknowledgment and acceptance of my spiritual gifts, allowing the possibility that through me they could help millions of spiritual seekers on the planet.

For three weeks I became aware of a hawk on my property. First, it killed and ate a bird on my upstairs balcony. The following day it killed and ate another bird at my front door. It killed a third time in my backyard a few days later. That hawk certainly got my attention. I realized there must a Spiritual meaning or message to what was happening.

I researched the meaning, seeking answers. Here is what I discovered, *"Stop doubting your ideas and assert yourself. Trust in your instincts and feelings. Have confidence in any bright ideas that have recently come into mind."*

One of the greatest gifts a hawk totem person can give the world is their vision of a better, brighter future. Visionaries are always ahead of their time and it is not easy seeing what other totem animal people are unwilling to see. Many messages hawk totems bring are about freeing yourself of limiting thoughts and beliefs which dampen your Spirit's ability to soar above your life, gaining a greater perspective. This ability to soar high above and catch a glimpse of the bigger picture allows Hawk-Spirit people to survive and flourish. What I find fascinating about the timing of these visits is we just had the spring equinox when it occurred the most recent time. For the last two nights I was awakened at 3:33 AM in the morning, of course. I called on Kwan Yin, the Ascended Master who works with me. As I lay there in the wee hours, pulsating, vibrating and waiting, it finally happened on the last night.

When I went to bed I was guided to clear my space, so I did. By now you know I was intensely pulsating and vibrating. My heart was beating in my head so loudly, it was difficult sleeping. Eventually I fell asleep. At the stroke of 3:33 AM in the morning, I awoke, calling on Kwan Yin again. I was guided to enter into prayer, so I did. My body felt like it disappeared, but I knew I was there because I still heard my heart beating in my head.

I looked up, and saw a magnificent, bright, emerald green light hovering overhead. One of my guides, my integration guide, was present. The energy was powerful as they shared the information I indeed had reached the level of Christ Consciousness. I was ready to soar to new heights. The old me was gone. I was one in this space with the pulsating, the vibrating, and my heart beating in my head for another entire hour.

Then it grew quiet. My heart no longer beat in my head like a drum. The pulsating and vibrating dropped to a bearable level. The green light moved out of my line of vision. In the stillness of the moment I knew I was finally ready to do the work for which I was born. Doubts or fears would no longer hold me back.

To help me fully embrace my spiritual gifts, abilities and soul purpose I remembered again, one morning during a lucid dream, I found myself sitting in a classroom. The teacher asked me to answer a question and complete a project. Instead I got up and said, "I no longer need to do that." I began singing all my life lessons learned. I recounted each and every one. I realized my schooling was complete. I was ready to graduate and I left the classroom.

Shortly afterward, one evening following my meditation, I heard a high-pitched sound and saw a dazzling burst of golden, white light. Standing in front of me was a magnificent golden androgynous being, the future me, my God-Self. This future me came because I was finally in alignment with my true, authentic, soul purpose.

In short, you must determine your soul purpose, then discover how best to fulfill it while not sacrificing your soul. If you fulfill your purpose, but realize you cannot stand who you have become, you may regret the journey. Using spiritual enlightenment to fulfill your soul purpose will insure living at one with peace regarding the steps you have taken to accomplish your personal purpose.

No one can tell you your soul purpose. You must seek to discern it through internal reflection and self-discovery. In essence, your soul purpose is about utilizing whatever abilities you have to accomplish important tasks and goals with your life.

Chapter Ten:

You Are The Light

"The greatest thing you can do for another is not just to share your riches, but to reveal to them their own."

~~ BENJAMIN DISRAELI

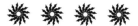

SO MANY PEOPLE EXPERIENCE THEMSELVES AS SEPARATE BEINGS:

- Separate from each other
- Separate from God and from the physical Universe.

There is No Separation

From this viewpoint of separation it is impossible to perceive the true nature of who you truly are; of matter, energy, and, the life force in everything you have labeled "God." I believe as you dig deeper into the true nature of "reality" it will become clear the separation of body, mind, and Spirit is an illusion. These are simply aspects of one thing or being. As Spiritual beings, we must take a closer look, understanding and applying this information in our everyday lives. We are not weak, sinful, shameful human creatures who must somehow earn the right to become spiritual beings. We are spiritual beings having a human experience. That is a 180-degree swing in perception as compared to formalized religious belief systems which support the false notion you must earn your way back to something or someplace. Indeed, it changes everything.

The metamorphosis commenced. I morphed beyond the chrysalis, broke free of my "shell" and was becoming the butterfly. As I continued traversing this experience called "awakening" I noticed how many "awakened people" harped on and on about religion. I have come to realize it does not matter what religion you practice, or, if you practice any religion at all. Every belief system is part of "The House of Universal Spirituality." You simply have moved from one room to another, but both systems are in the same house.

Be Open to Truth

I suggest recognizing the air is the same, as is the space, the light and the walls of each room. All religions contain some truths as well as a degree of ignorance or falsehoods. Getting stuck in ignorance or falsehoods and throwing out the baby with the bath water and believing all religious and spiritual philosophies are false or corrupt is choosing to remain asleep. Your divine knowledge or truths are the awakening, in my humble opinion. It is unnecessary to pigeon-hole yourself in a box marked with a specific religious label. Rather, be open to truth, whatever it may look like. The truth will faithfully set you free. As the human race, we should use our right to question everything and reject logic in discovering the truth.

As a person seeking your own spiritual awakening you are probably beginning to recognize the divine is within each of us. You no longer need to seek your connectedness from an outside viewpoint. Your best, most honest, vantage point is actually on the inside: it always was and always will be inside each one of us.

As the Bible in Luke 17:21 says, *"The kingdom of heaven is within."* You may need a little prodding to remember this message at times. Along with seeing your true Higher-Self for the first time, as a result of reading this book, I hope you are beginning to see the world as it relates to the whole; knowing you are connected to the one Source, the God-Source. The process and development of expressing your spirituality and faith can have many faces throughout your lifetime.

Many people are beginning to understand spirituality must be experiential in nature to be fully understood. The disharmony and disconnect of organized religion with all its hard and fast rules and dogma was the vehicle by which transformation was supposed to evolve. As a people, we have forgotten we are part of the collective whole.

You may have always believed you must belong to a system of rigid rules to have value on the spiritual plane or simply as a person. Without even realizing it, you may believe there is something you must find, have, do or fulfill to be viewed as okay. You may not yet realize belonging to an "organization" made of this Earth, or this dimension, is momentary. It can leave you or you may leave it. Nothing you own here on Earth is forever, except the soul you carry around bringing life to your body.

I was being shown how real the non-physical is as it became second nature for me to move into it. I found myself in a golden, white place.

Jesus appeared for a moment with love and light surrounding him. Then he seemingly morphed into another man wearing an ancient, Roman-style uniform. He wore no armor, but wore a short, crimson tunic with leather trim and leather sandals. I did not feel it was the uniform of a servant; it seemed more official. However, it did appear a bit ill-fitting at the shoulders. This made me lighten up and smile. He had the biggest smile on his face, and, I began jumping up and down with excitement. I approached him and shook his hand, grasping it with both my hands. I felt it. Days prior to this experience I was hearing the name William. I knew intuitively this was he.

As I shook his hand and began a battery of questions, I started moving back through the vortex. With me was a brilliant, yellowish-green orb. My team came right in, along with my Higher-Self. They told me the "WILL" was energy. They also told me to say, *"I AM Love, I AM Light"* over and over. My body began swaying as if I were floating on water. When I stopped the mantra the movement stopped. I kept repeating it and each time the movement happened. I asked them what it meant and was told we must be in the ebb and flow of the energy that creates. He is the "WILL" part of the I AM of Will I AM or William. The action part makes all things manifest. I was given the Will of the I AM to use. I had to experiment with this new-found ability.

A few nights later, I said I wanted to move through space at will. My team returned and told me to chant once again. Using my inner voice I began chanting, "I *AM love, I AM Light,*" until I became aware my body was dematerializing. I moved into space and saw myself in my Merkaba, my chariot. Instantly I knew I was on a different planet in a parallel life of mine. I knew I was her and she knew she was me as well. We sat and spoke, until she told me it was time to return. I replied, "I know." Then I felt and saw myself move back through the vortex and back into my bed.

The next evening I tried to re-create the experience, but mid-way I had to use the bathroom. When I got up I fell, because my left leg was gone. I was already dematerializing while awake and aware.

You Are Perfect, Whole and Complete

You are already part of a Higher Power, no matter what name you attach to it; God, Buddha, Mohammed, Yahweh or Great Spirit. If great power already exists within us, we do not have to go anywhere. Instead begin by going within. Listen to that still, small voice and get to know yourself. In that way you will find yourself already perfect, whole and complete. Anything appearing contrary to this, whether an illness or lack can be easily adjusted back to perfection.

Believe you are a divine being; here to expand and grow in whatever way seems best for you. Knowing your divinity is perfect. As a spiritual being, live your life with love and respect and you cannot get it wrong. God made everything and it is good. Why would he make you and me and then tell us we are bad from the moment of our birth?

We are good, because it only makes sense. True awakening is an ever-changing landscape, and a new way of thinking and believing. In fact, your conscious awakening changes with every new thing you learn about yourself and how you want to live your life. It grows and expands with you, and, you grow and expand with it.

Spirit: Feeding and Challenging You

Spirituality should feed your Spirit and inspire you to eagerly discover more about this amazing journey called life and death. It should also challenge you to think for yourself instead of letting others tell you what you should think, feel or believe. Spirit should feed you, filling you up and making you feel good, loved, happy and content. It should not condemn you, making you feel guilty.

Of course, we all want to belong to something. Belongingness is part of our nature. However, instead of belonging to an organization that controls you, consider belonging to something which frees and empowers you. Belong to yourself and no other. True enlightenment comes from years of work altering your perspective and your perceptions regarding the world around you.

You may have read this world is an illusion. To a certain degree, this is true. The world itself is not an illusion; your perception of the world around you is the true illusion. Remain diligent and open to your path towards enlightenment and your worldview about what is real and what is an illusion. Your worldview will shift and change. You will discern fact from fiction: from what you hear on the evening news, and what is presented as news online, to whatever the popular belief is at that time. You may discover what you held close to your heart as true is not necessarily so. These things are part of the illusion you must overcome with time and reflection.

Look Beyond the Illusion

Look beyond the illusion to discover your own reality. When you find reality you may become a bit disappointed or dismayed. At this point in your development, you may experience a challenge when it comes to facing the magnitude of the illusion. You may choose to turn away from your path of awakening rather than face the ugly truth.

To attain spiritual enlightenment you must shed many so-called "truths" you currently hold dear. As you research more, you will discover you have been lied to about the world in which we live. You will learn about lies fed to us by government leaders, business leaders, religious leaders, educational leaders, the news media and more. Eventually they will all be stripped bare like the emperor with no clothes.

To truly grow in Spirit, you must realize every time you discover and shed a lie, you will gain a truth. I believe this shift or movement is what your growth is all about. This is part of the process called, "transmutation."

You must shed the old skin to embrace your emergence into your new, more open reality. Every truth you gain will serve to alter your previous perceptions, giving you clarity on your path to personal wisdom. Most people are satisfied living with comfortable, well-worn lies. But, as one who works to achieve spiritual mastery, you must have the courage to uncover the truth and accept the truth, no matter how ugly it may appear at first. Only in accepting truth and shedding the illusions of created lies will you find and embrace your own real freedom.

You will find the spiritual path is primarily a solitary venture. It is not a group activity, like most organized religions. You must summon the courage and determination to become your own authority. Initially, this concept may be incomprehensible if you have been programmed in the ways of a church, synagogue, mosque or temple. But it is a concept you must embrace to move forward knowing who you are and why you are here.

This does not mean you cannot, or should not associate with like-minded people. It means no matter what your associations with others, your growth is totally dependent on you. Only you can set your pace, your goals and develop your personal connection to God. No one can dictate what is right on your path to greater spiritual awareness. Only you and Spirit can decide for you. None of us has traveled exactly the same path, or had the same experiences, in this life or past lives. We each have aspects and foibles of our own to overcome. How you accomplish this feat will be unique to your experience.

A process that works for one person, may not work for another. So, do not get discouraged when you try something in spiritual practices touted by others as useful, and it does not work for you at all. You will surely encounter instances like these. There is no one true way; there never has been. You have the absolute right to walk your spiritual path any way you choose.

This is the greatest lie of organized religions; each one believes and professes itself as the one and only true way to God or enlightenment. To grow and expand, you must realize the error in such a claim by any and every religion.

Also, there are no Messiahs. No one is coming to save you. Every Messiah was a spiritual master whose message was completely misunderstood by the masses of people who lived at the time. People who had no spiritual insight or wisdom to understand the essence of their teachings. Religions were born and continue rebirthing.

If you want a Messiah or Savior, I suggest looking in the mirror. After all, you already know you possess God within. The reflection of self is the only Savior each of us will ever need. No one is going to wave a magic wand, bringing you spiritual enlightenment.

God will not gift you with spiritual wisdom and understanding unless you do the work unfolding and expanding. These are spiritual truths you can embrace and live with through the ups and downs of life and your adventure toward Spirit. In Ephesians 2:10 the Bible says, "We are his workmanship created in Christ Jesus." Within us and only within us, through our love and life, lie solutions. We will bring God to the earth again.

In John 8:32 the writer says, *"And ye shall know the truth, and the truth shall make you free."*

Created in God's Image

Love is the key to your awakening. In love, all fear, doubt and other obstacles that may cross your path will dissipate and be transmuted. The truth is we were created to become like Jesus Christ, nothing less. From the origins of our existence on planet earth as humans, God planned your return to your Christed state. This is your destiny. God announced this intention at the original creation. In Genesis 1:26 it is written God said, "Let us make human beings in our image, in our likeness." In all creation, only human beings are made "in God's image."

This is a great privilege and gives us dignity. However, most people allow false programming and outside influences, from organized religions to society at large, to strip us of this innate knowingness. We do not understand all this statement covers, but we do know some aspects it includes: Like God, we are spiritual beings. Our Spirits are immortal and will outlast our earthly bodies. We are intellectual, with the ability to think, reason and solve problems. Also like God, we are relational. We can give and receive genuine love. Finally, we have a moral conscience, and we can discern right from wrong.

What is needed most is the full commitment of your heart to a way of life and a way of thinking to sustain you in love, innocence and hope.

Without this commitment, the entrenched interests of the forces of separation have a greater effect. With this commitment, the strength of your heart and soul will find a way of sustaining you, no matter what circumstances pop up. To discover this freedom, release, or shift the lies, and false programming you may have heard your entire life. These things no longer serve your highest and best good. You must be aware of the illusions forced upon you all day and night by those who intend to keep you mentally enslaved and subservient to their illusion.

As you gain more truth, you gain more strength, provided you have the courage to see the truth and not let lies keep you dwelling in fear. Fear is the enemy of people on their spiritual path. Fear is the belief bad things will happen in the future. Pick your fear:

- Losing your friends
- Losing your family
- Losing your current religious faith

All these fears plague some seekers of truth. It is your choice to continue believing the illusion or not. Some people reading this book will not be strong enough, or spiritually hungry enough to surpass and grow beyond their fears. You may proceed only part of the way on your spiritual path, or, abandon it altogether. You will come to your own truths in your own time.

This journey has many twists and turns, just as I believed when my visits from inter-dimensional beings began. I was even visited by my first mother, known as the long haired people; a race of twelfth dimensional beings and an advanced race. I will never forget the love she felt for me. I look forward to moving through time and space to visit her at my far away home.

For now, the journey of awakening continues. There are more experiences to share with you, in time. As I look back upon the words written on these pages, I ponder the amazing journey I have been on and continue navigating. Expansion never ends.

I believe I have given you as clear a glimpse as I can in to my awakening experiences. I hope it encourages and inspires you to pursue your own awakening. I am reminded of the help and love I have received from the non-physical plane; my team and how they have guided me every step of the way. Those times when I was at a loss for words they seemed to always magically appear. My twelfth dimensional Mom came to me, just to show love and let me know I am not alone. She helped me change my perception of myself, and, she honors my dedication to fulfilling what I came here in this lifetime to do, my soul's purpose, a bridge between Heaven and Earth.

To my brother, Jesus, who has come every time something transfiguring has occurred to me with love and guidance. He even became William and the Will of the I AM to give me the will to create not only the life I desire but a desire to be of service. To Kwan Yin, Goddess of Mercy, indeed we must be compassionate to ourselves. The path is rocky at times. Kwan Yin energized my will to push onward.

I hope my book, "You're Not Crazy – You're Awakening!" has inspired you to reach the being of who you truly are. Be the light, and be the love. Stop for a moment and take a breath. You will see it has all been designed by you, to advance you on your path. I remind you to acknowledge, accept and give thanks. Learn, grow and continue on your journey into the light.

"Go confidently in the direction of your dreams.
Live the life you've imagined.
As you simplify your life,
the laws of the Universe will be simpler."

~~ HENRY DAVID THOREAU

46508874R00086

Made in the USA
Lexington, KY
06 November 2015